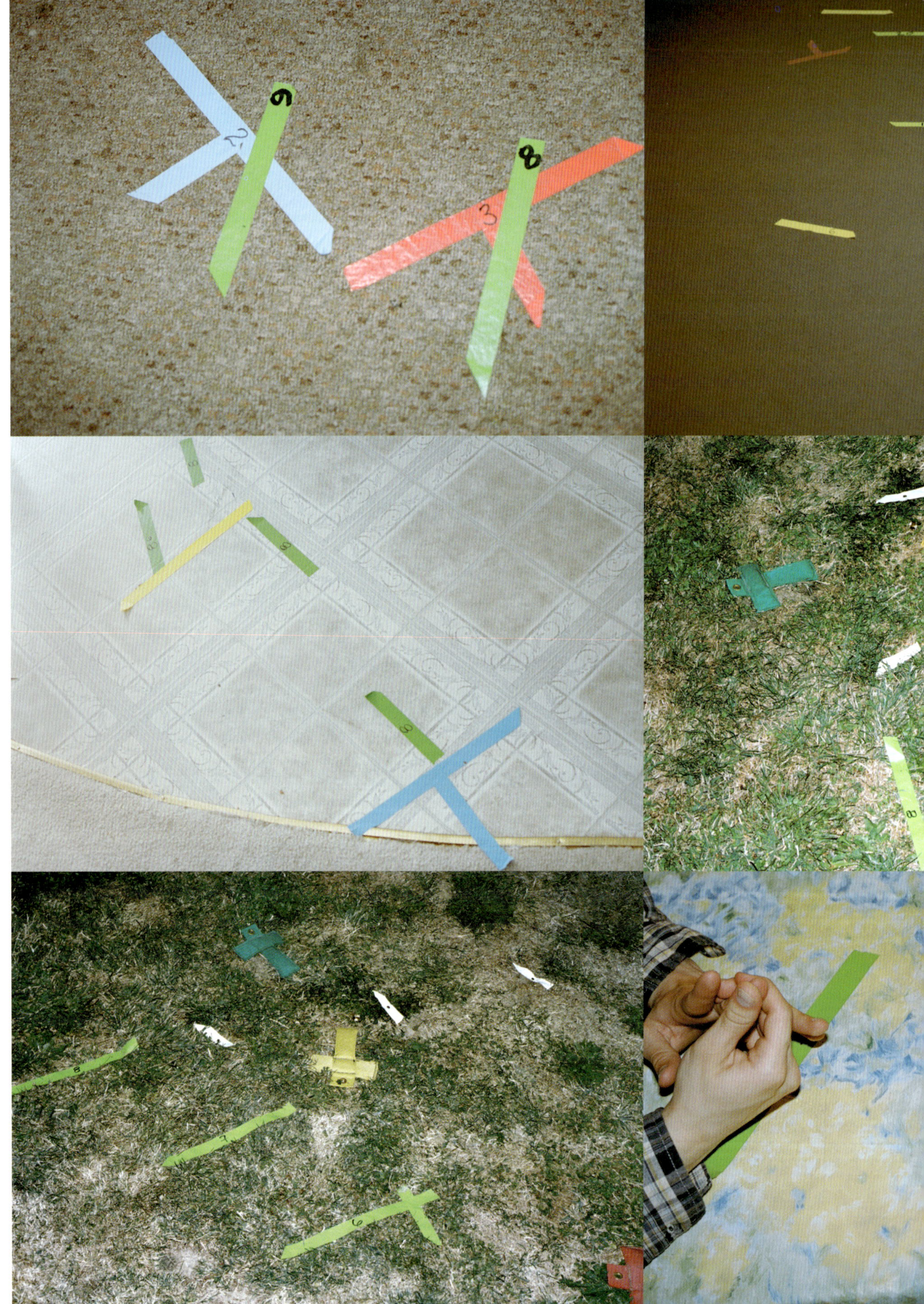

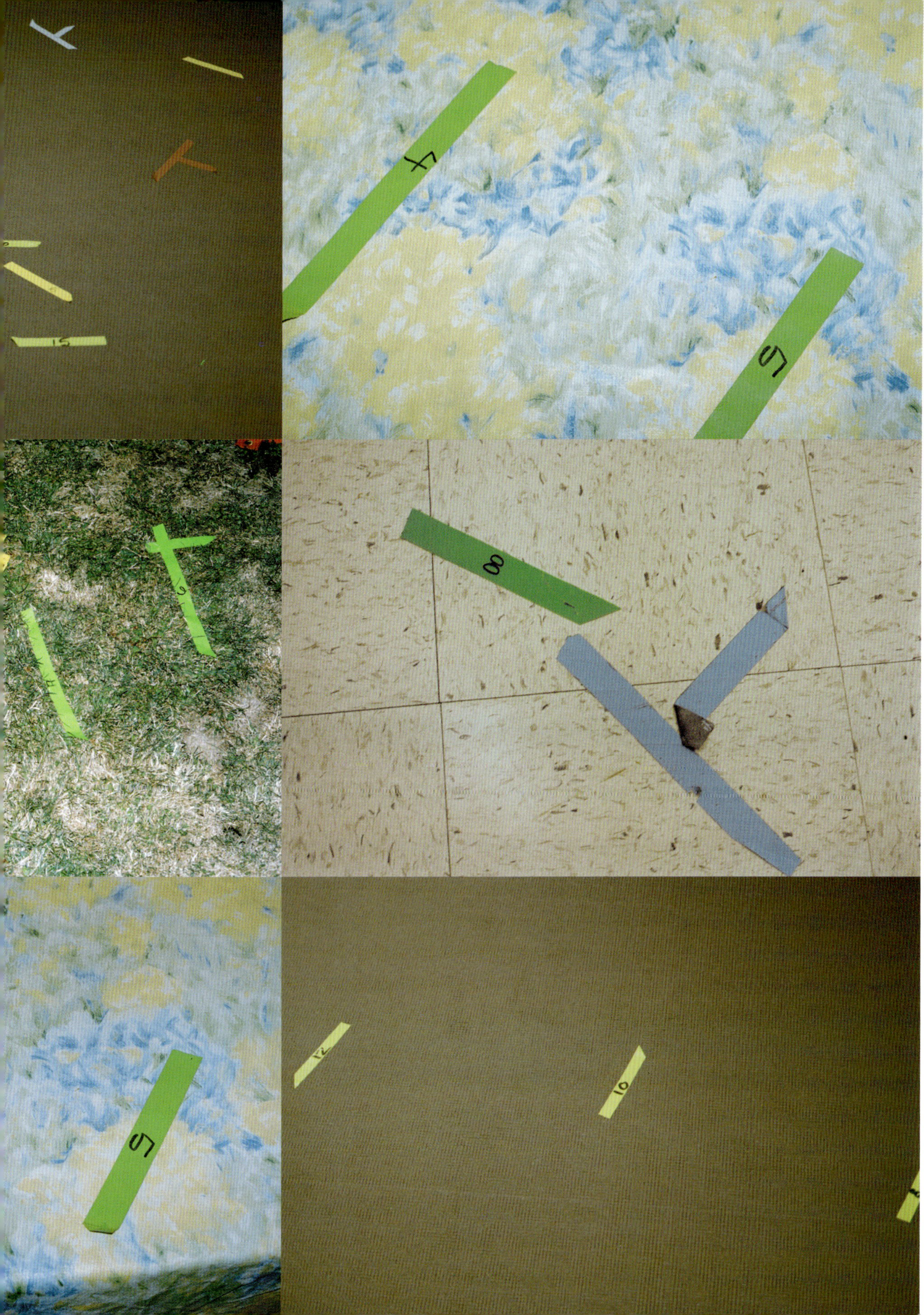

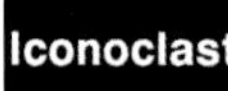
Iconoclast

THUMBSUCKER

PHOTOGRAPHY FROM THE FILM
BY MIKE MILLS

PHOTOGRAPHS BY

MARK BORTHWICK

TODD COLE

TAKASHI HOMMA

RYAN McGINLEY

ED TEMPLETON

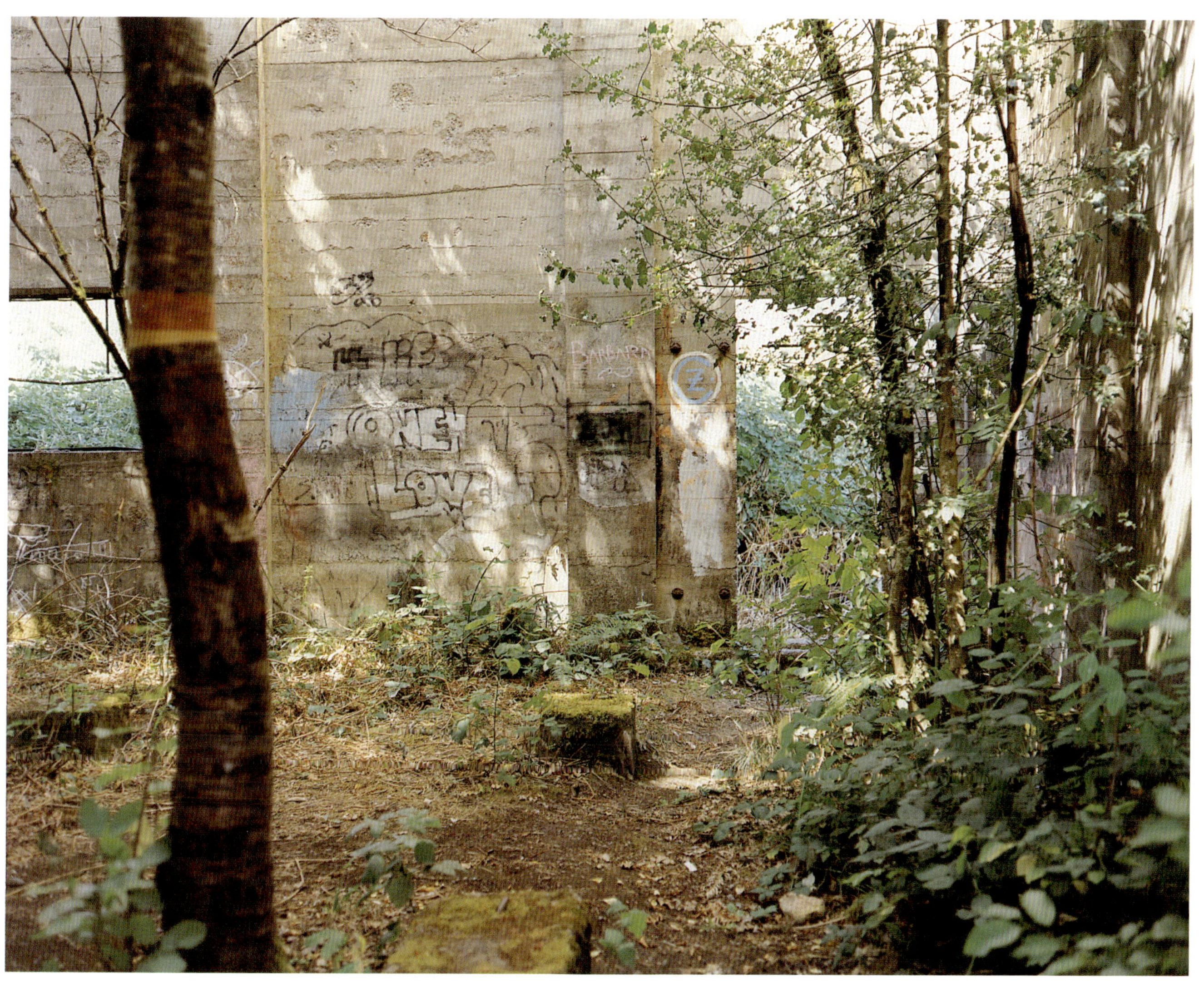

TH

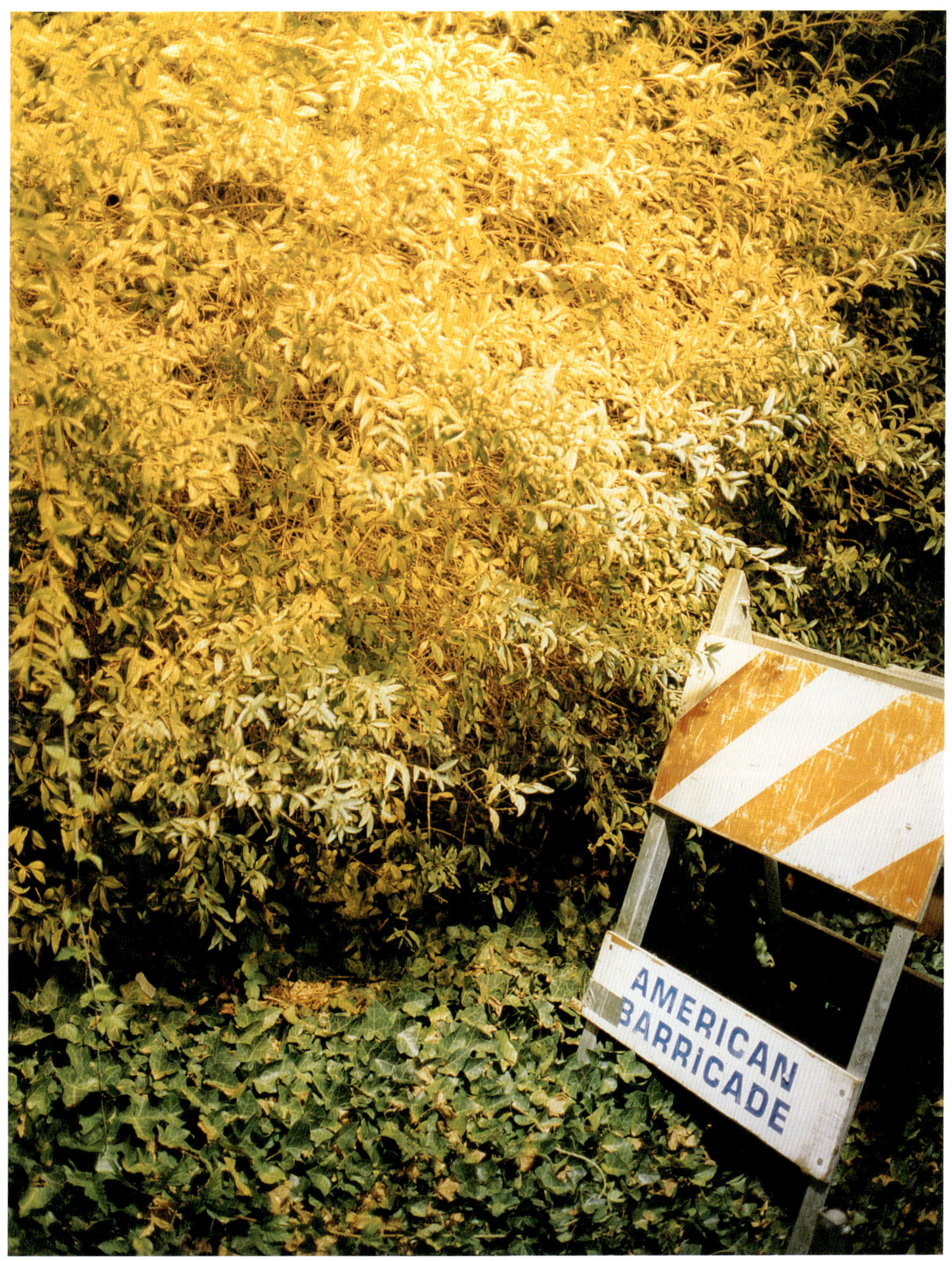

TH

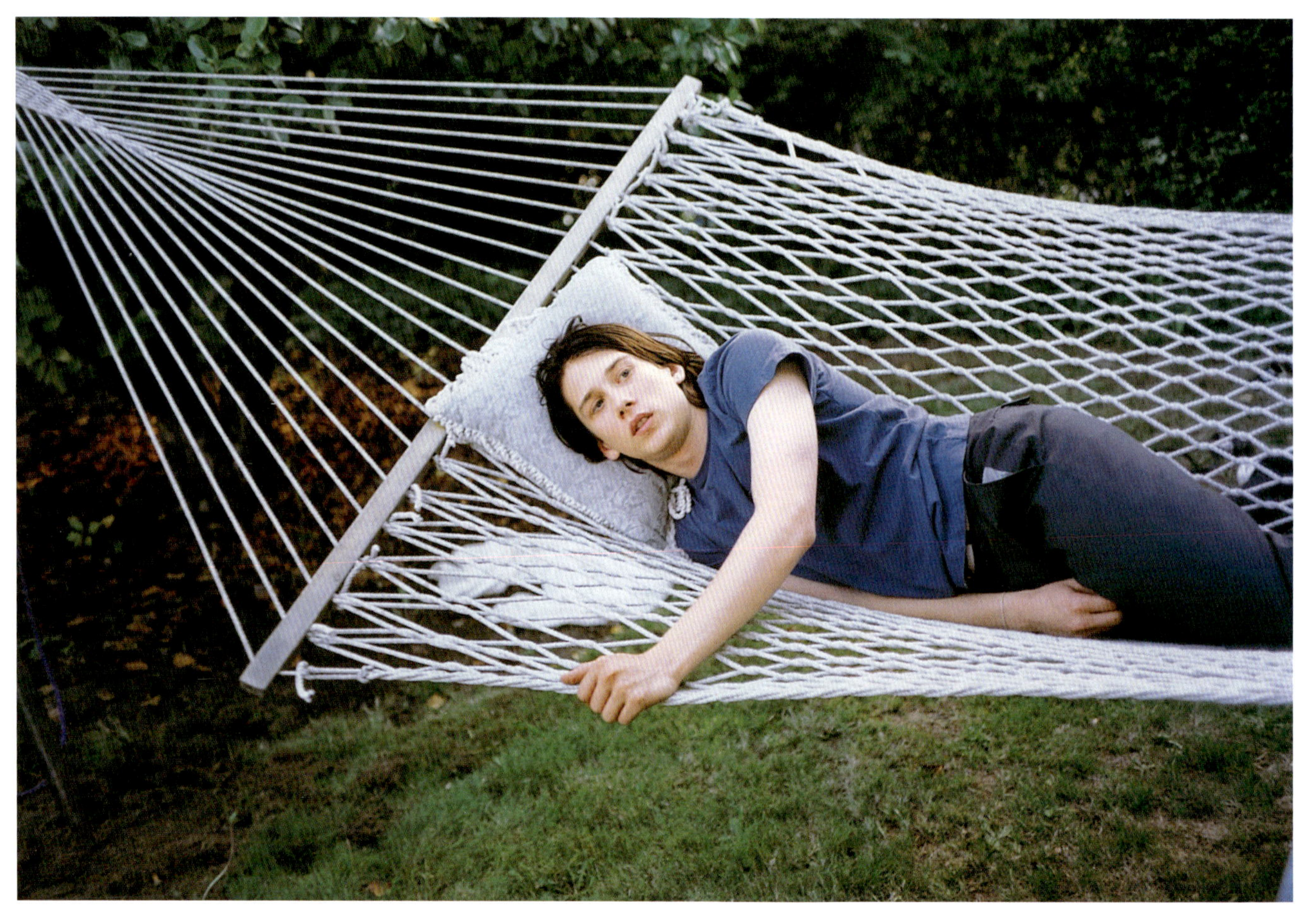

TH

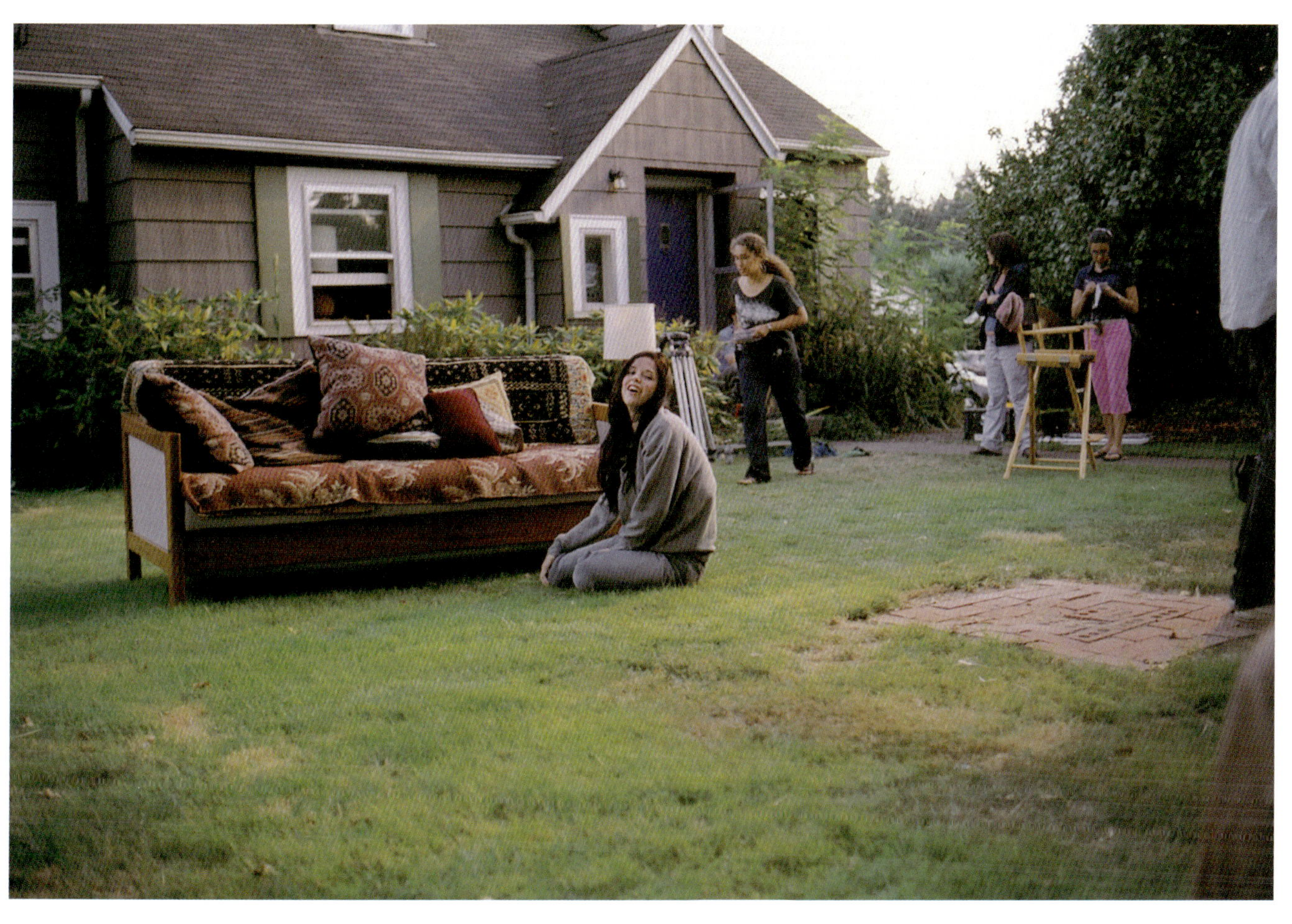

TH

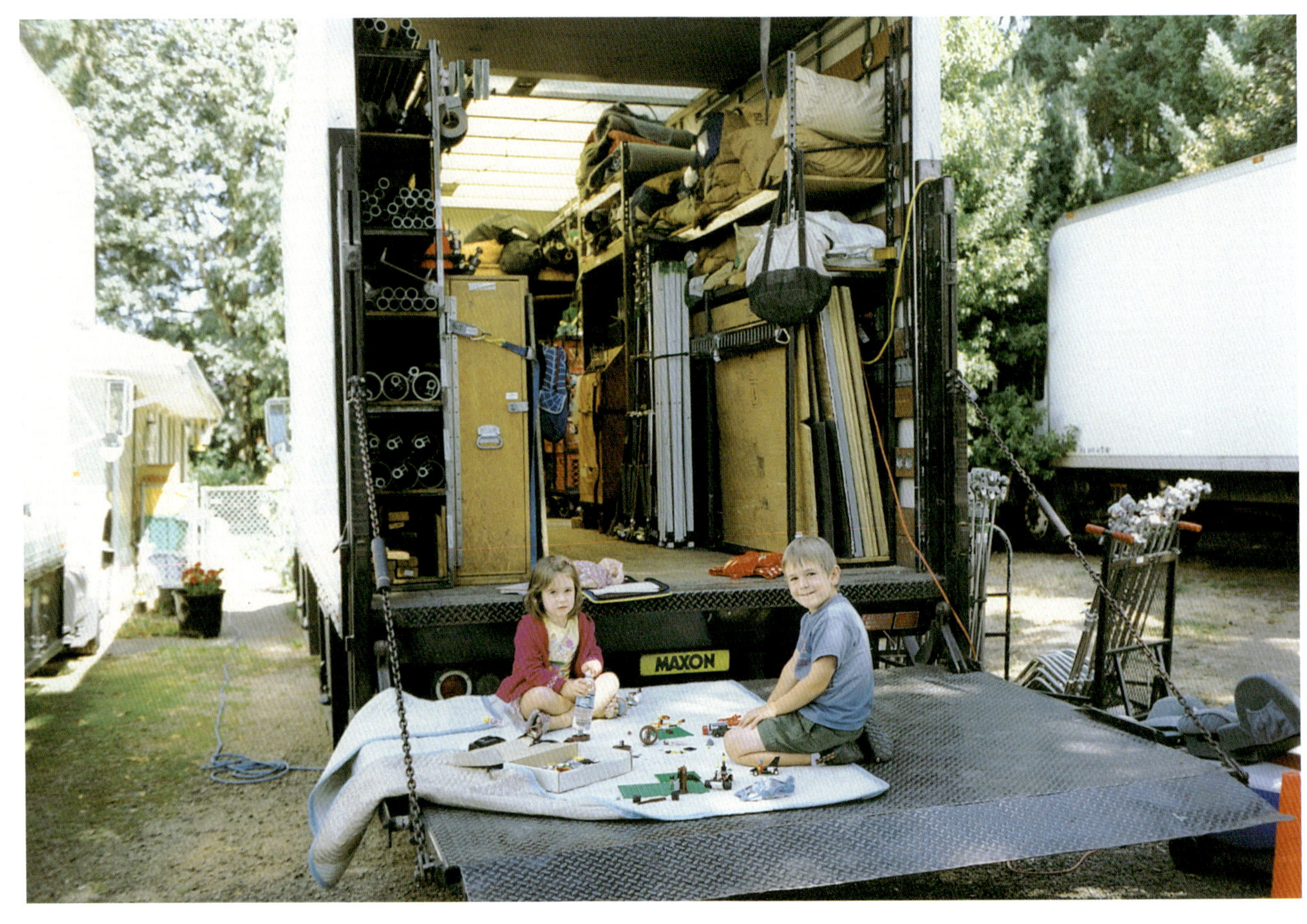

TH

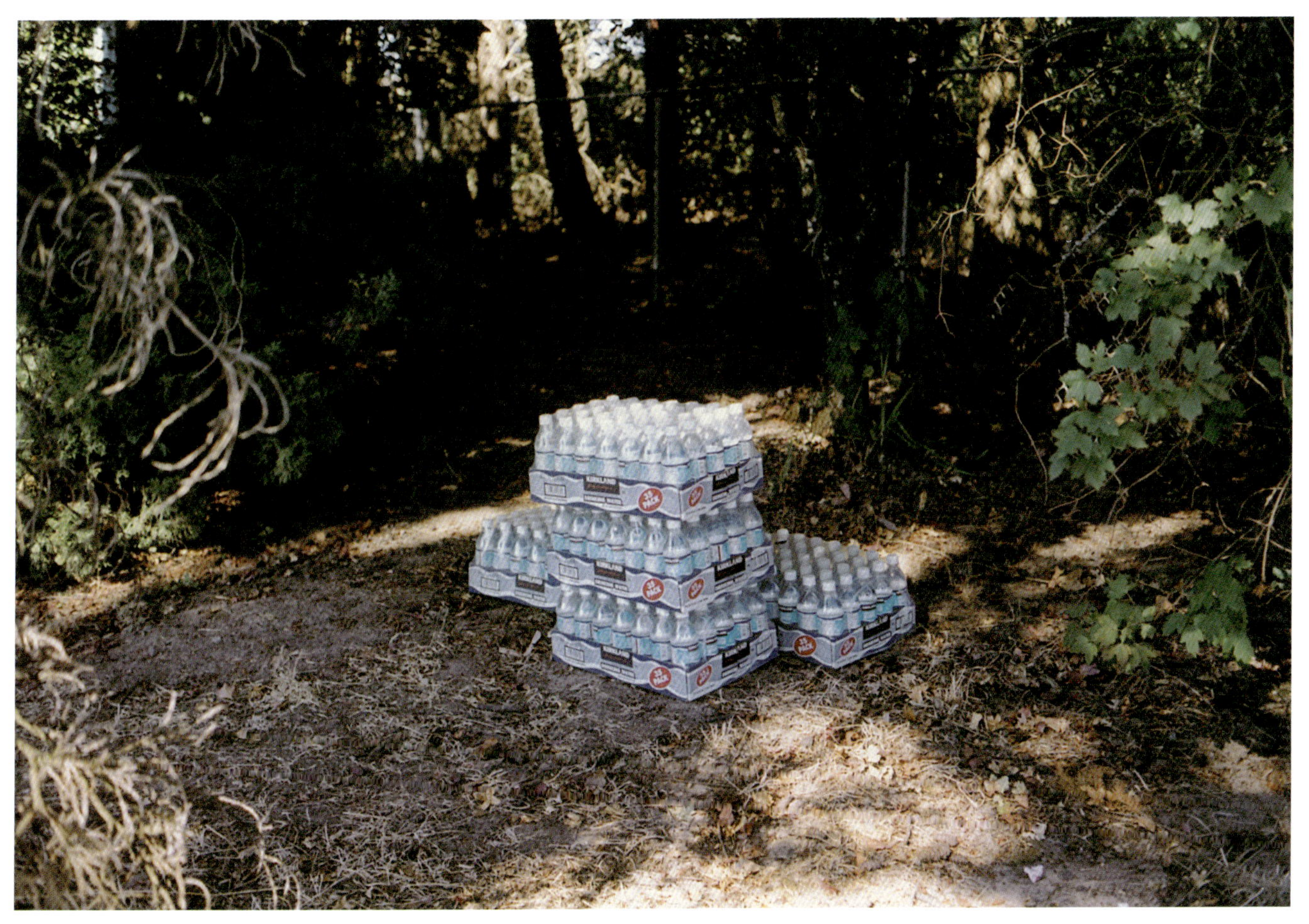

TH

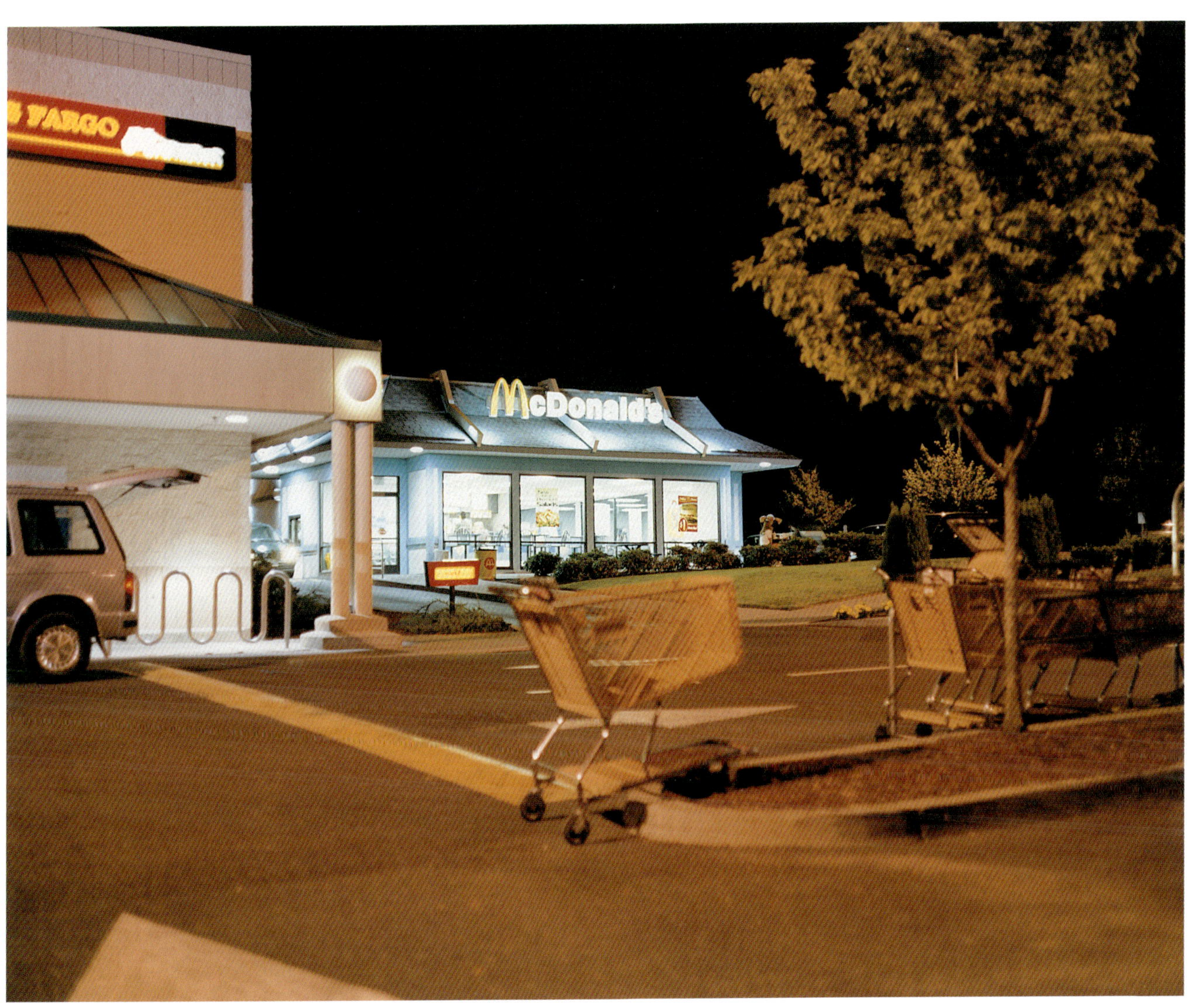

TH

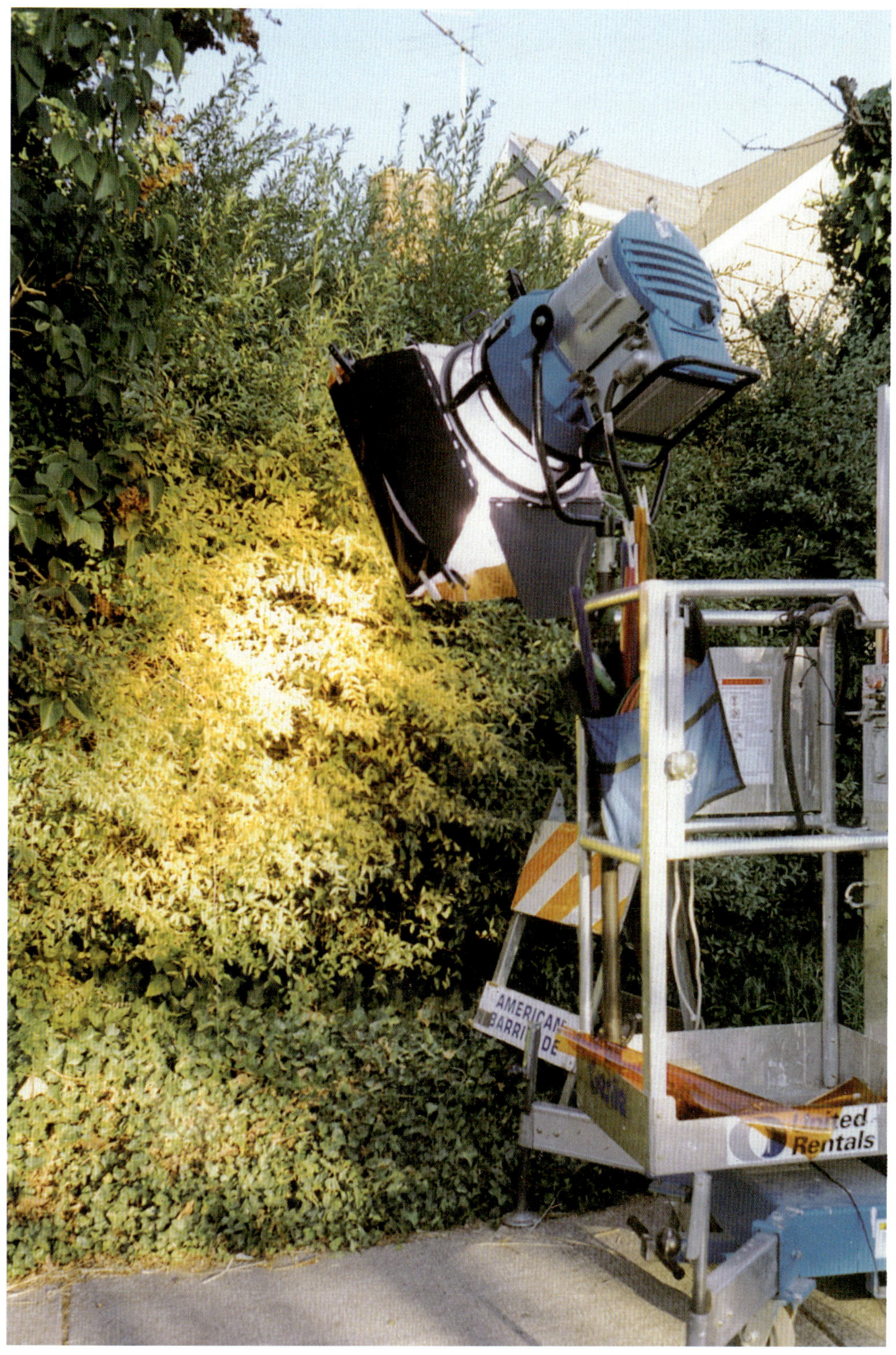

TH

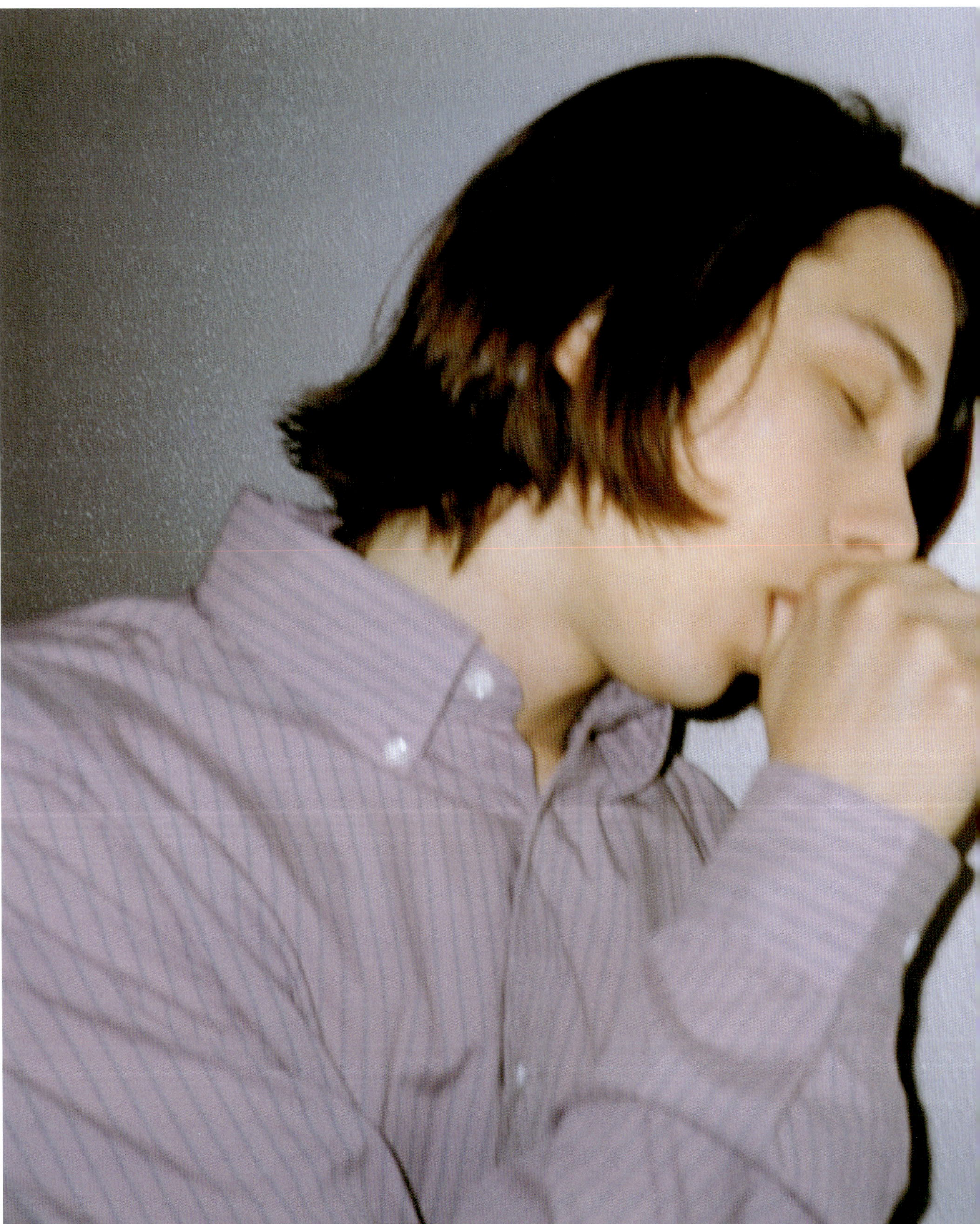

TH

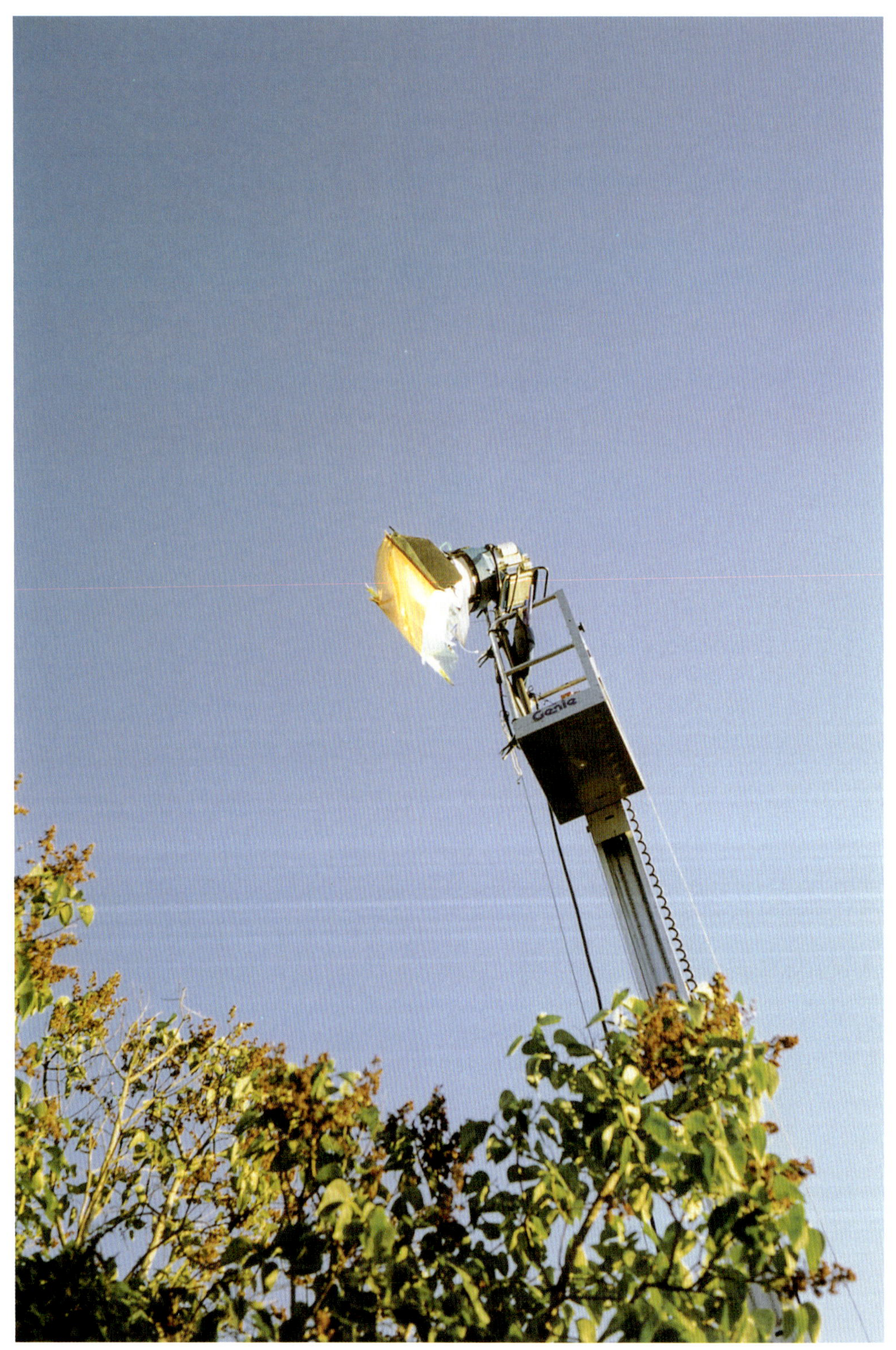

TH

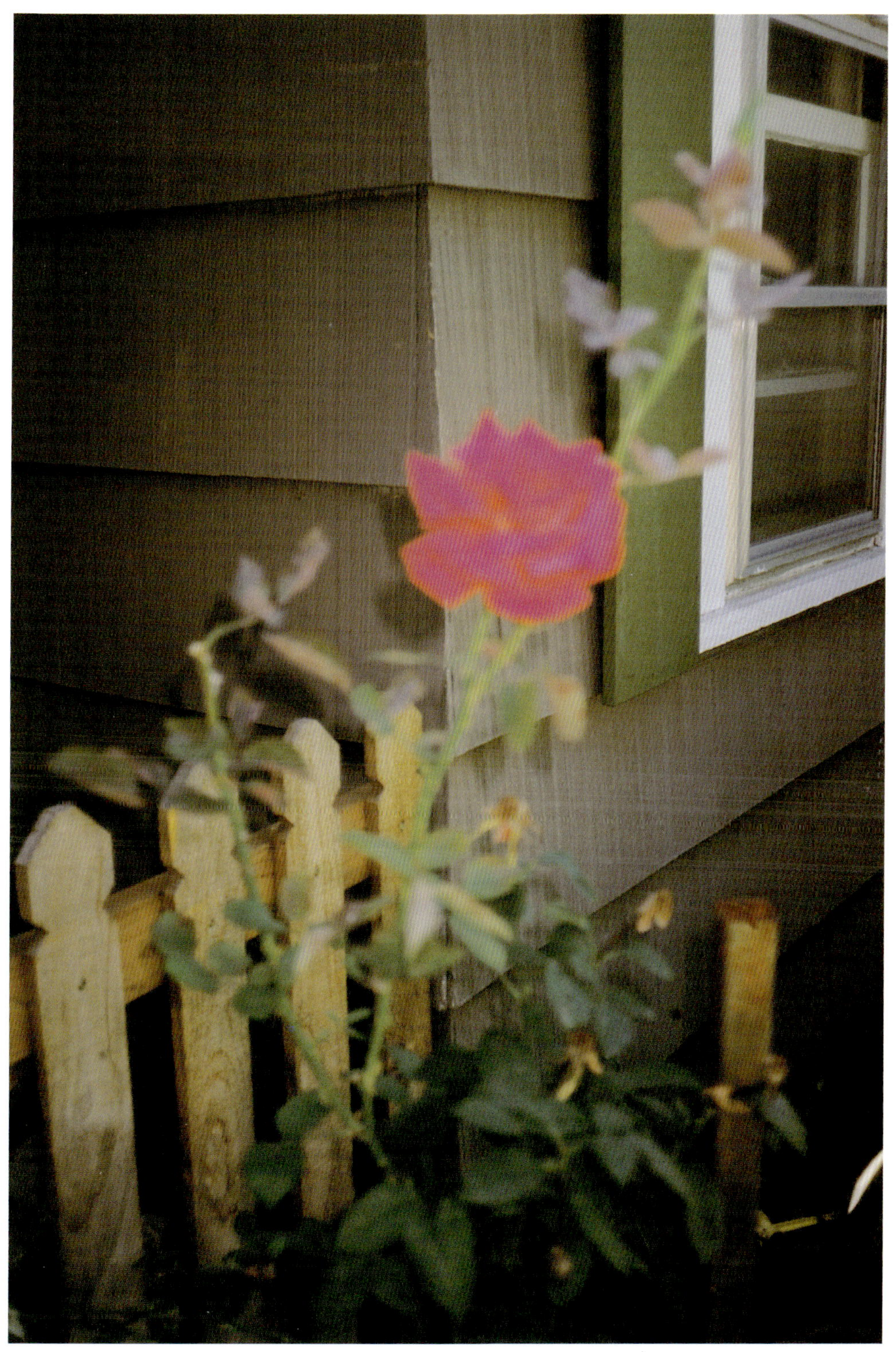

TH

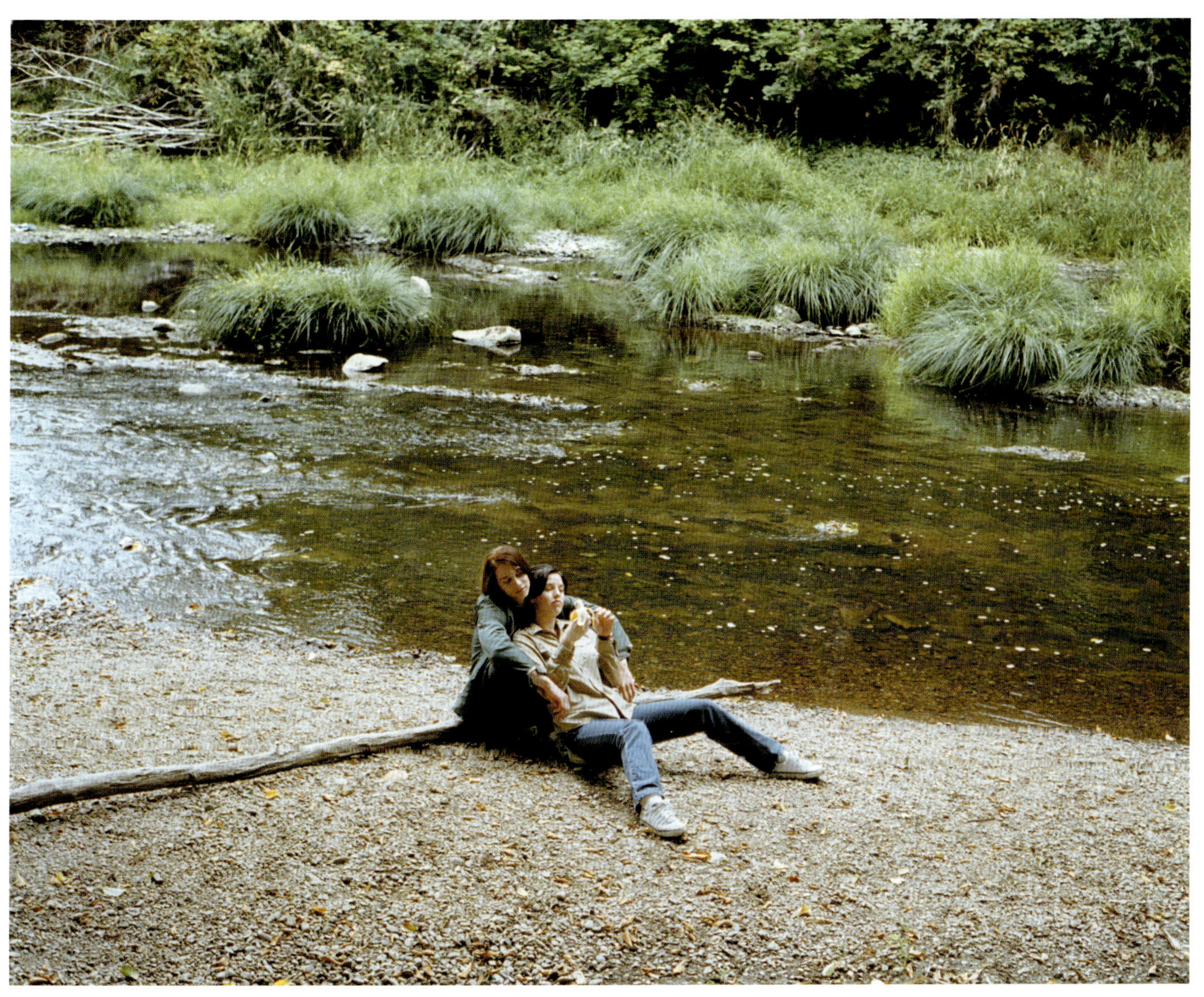

TC

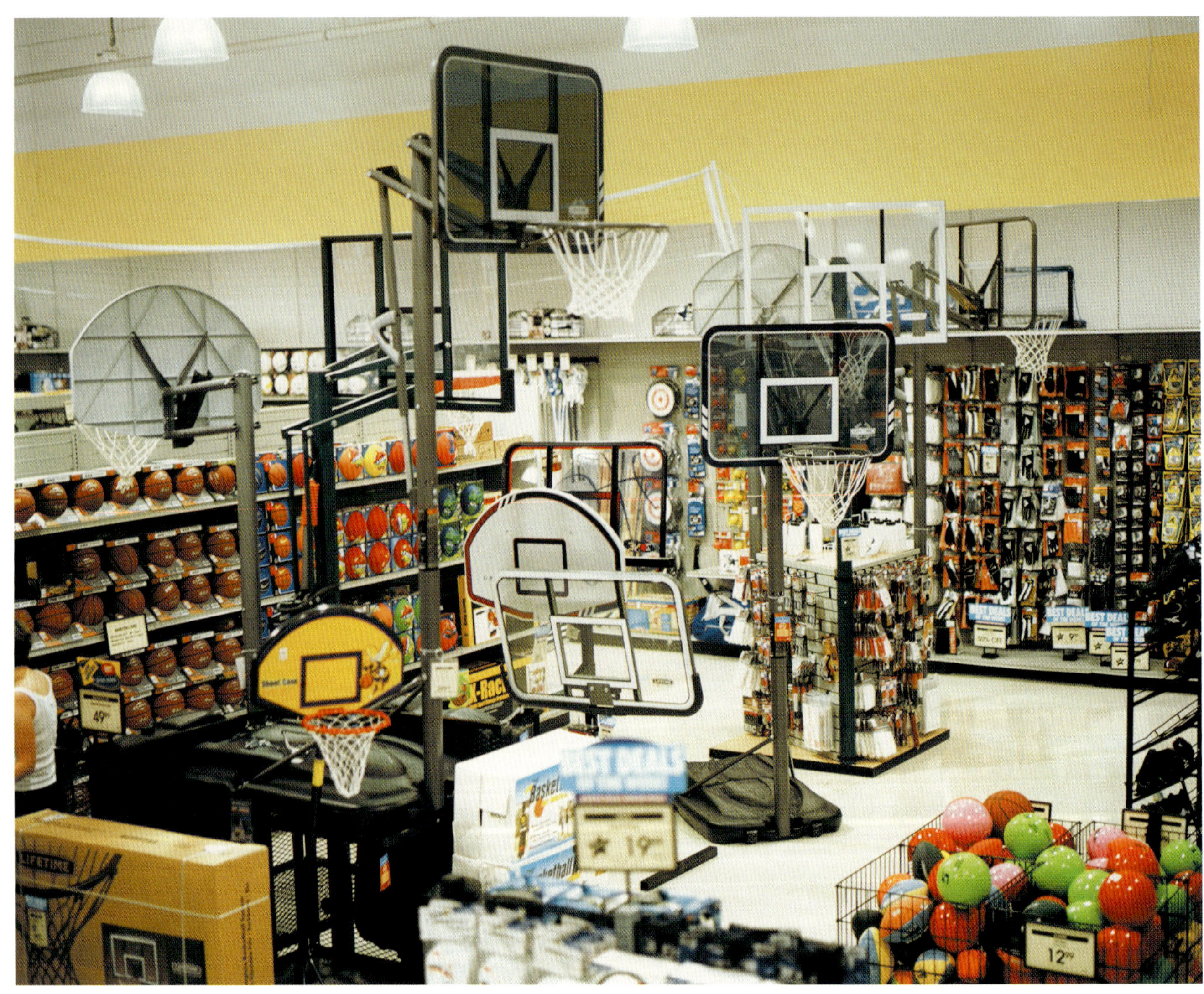

TC

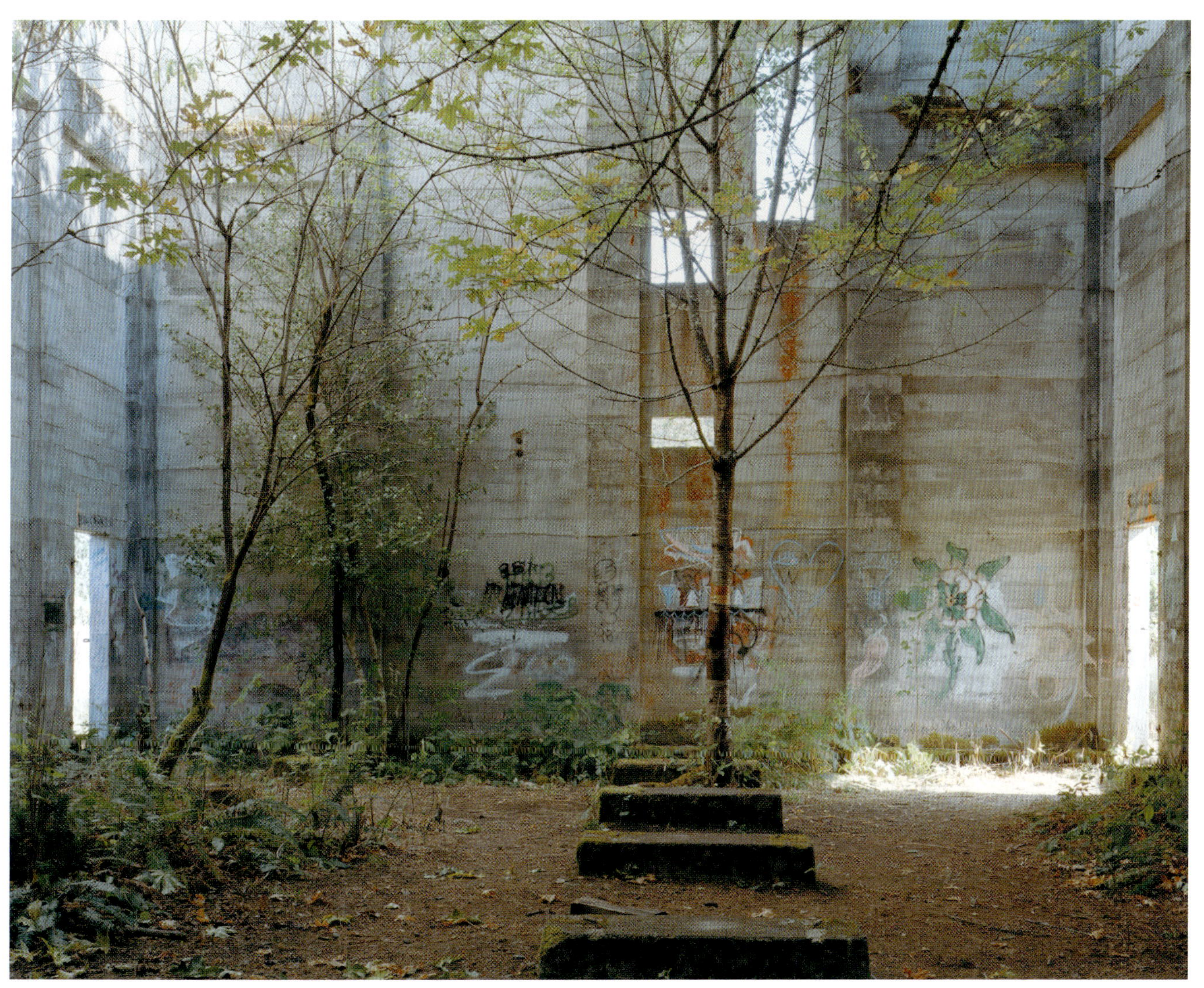

TC

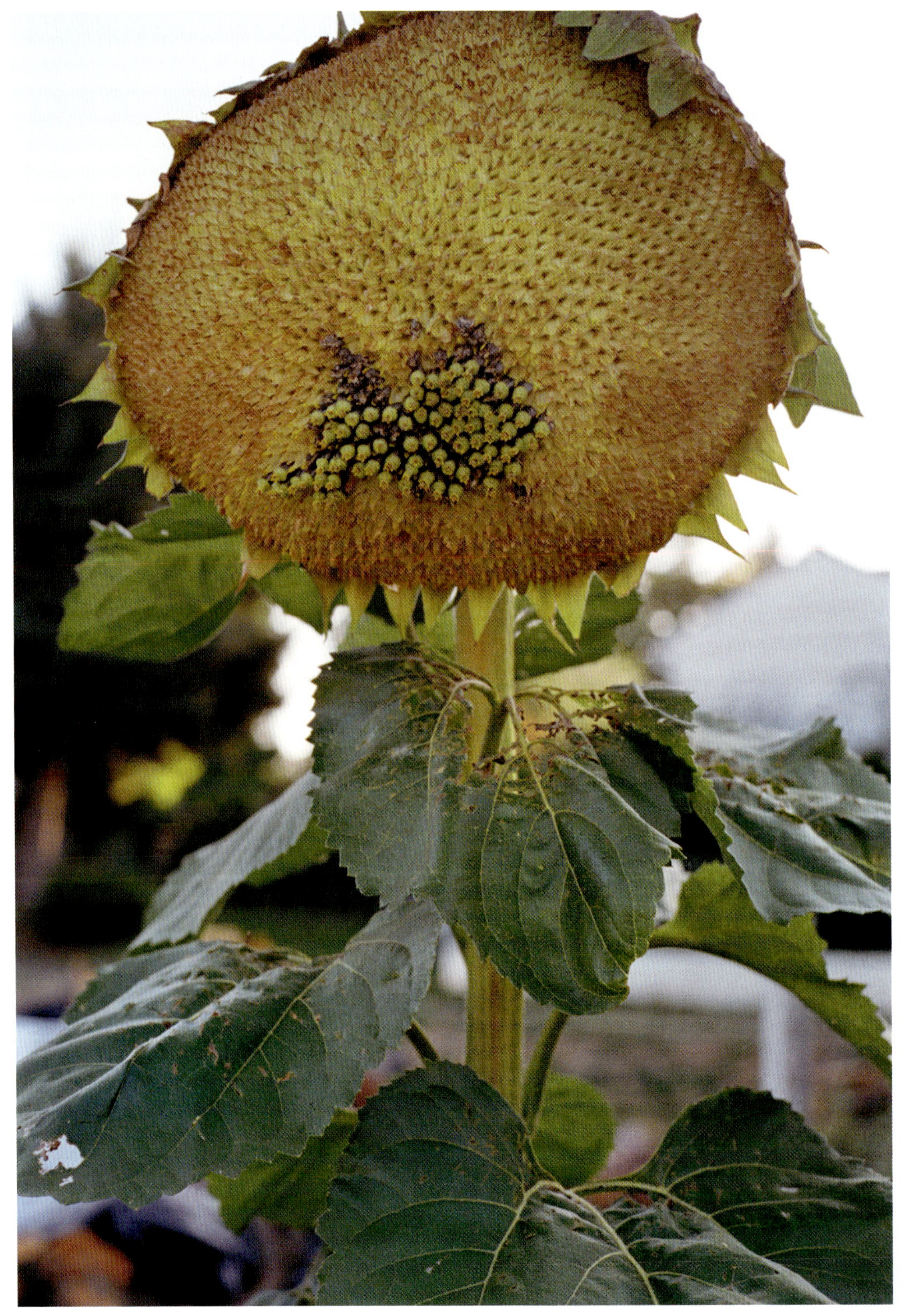

TC

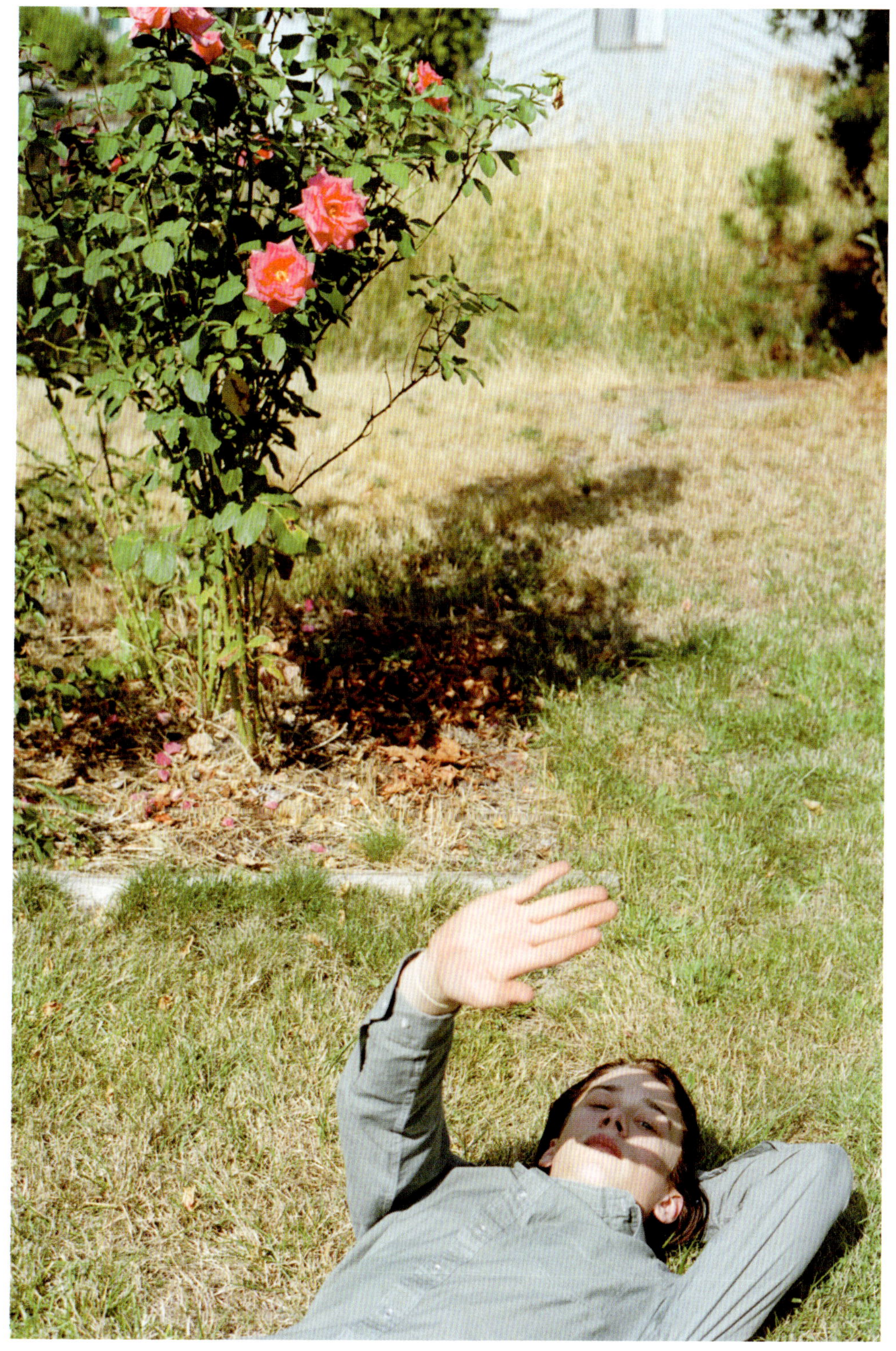

TC

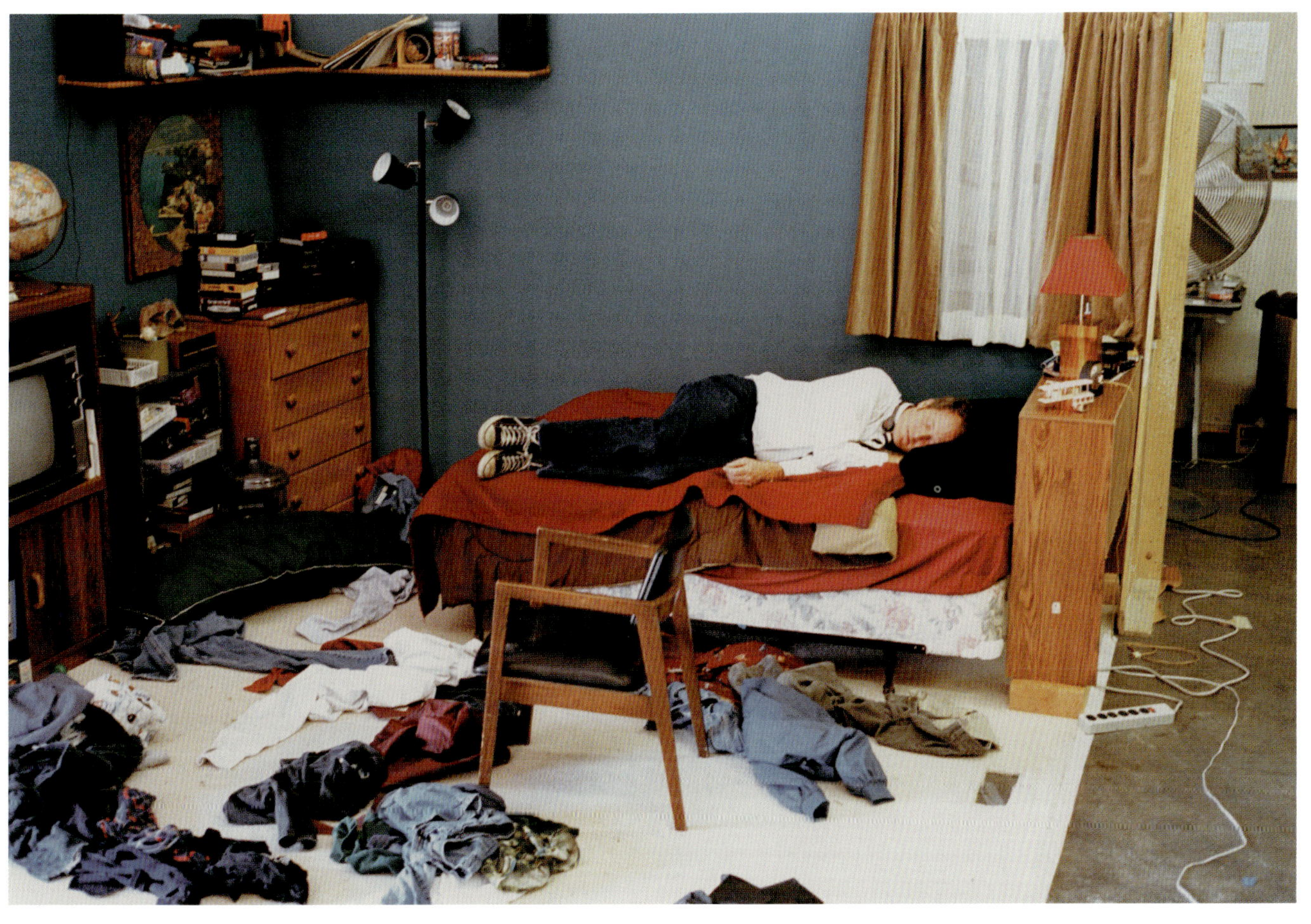

TC

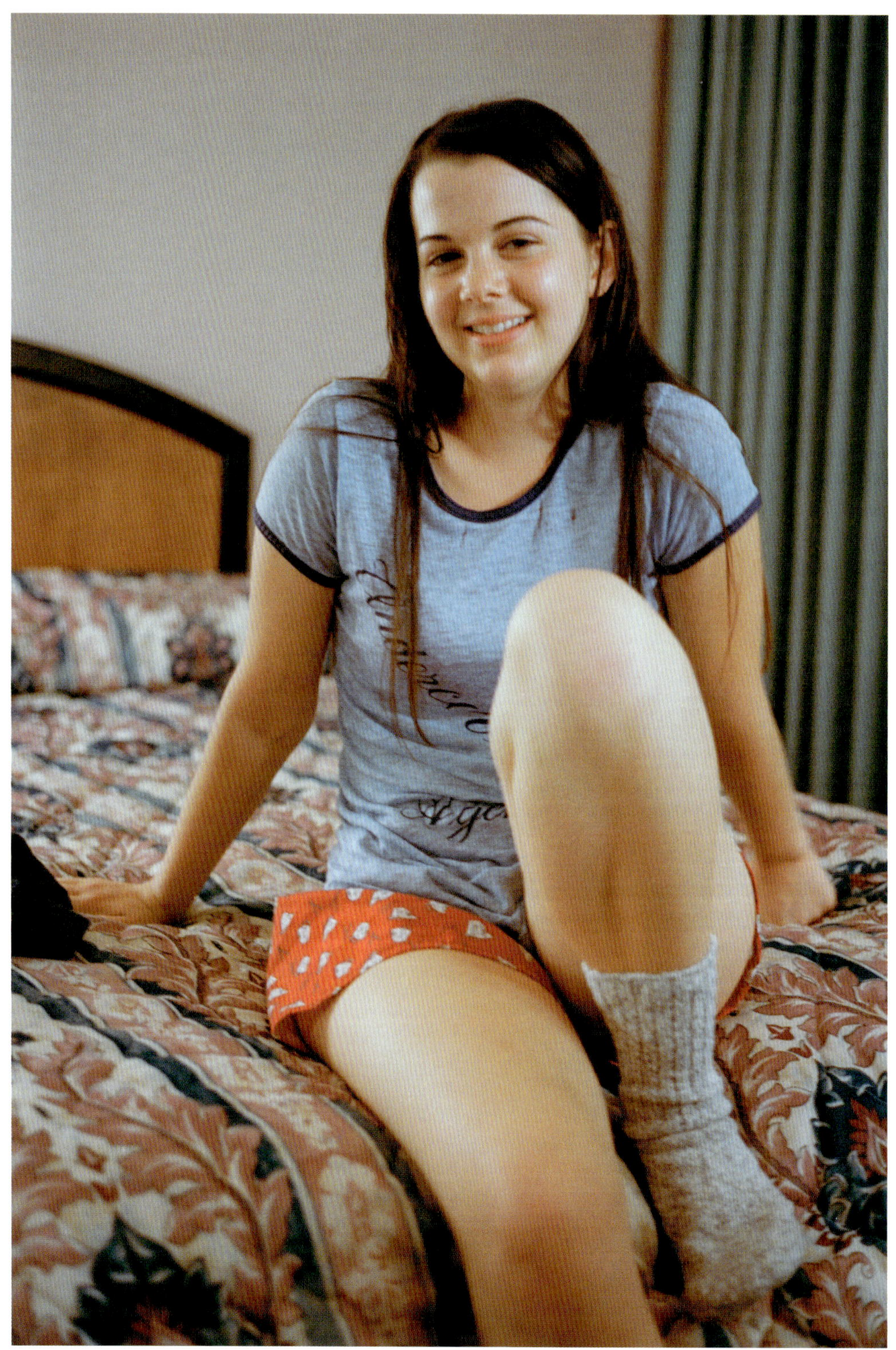

TC

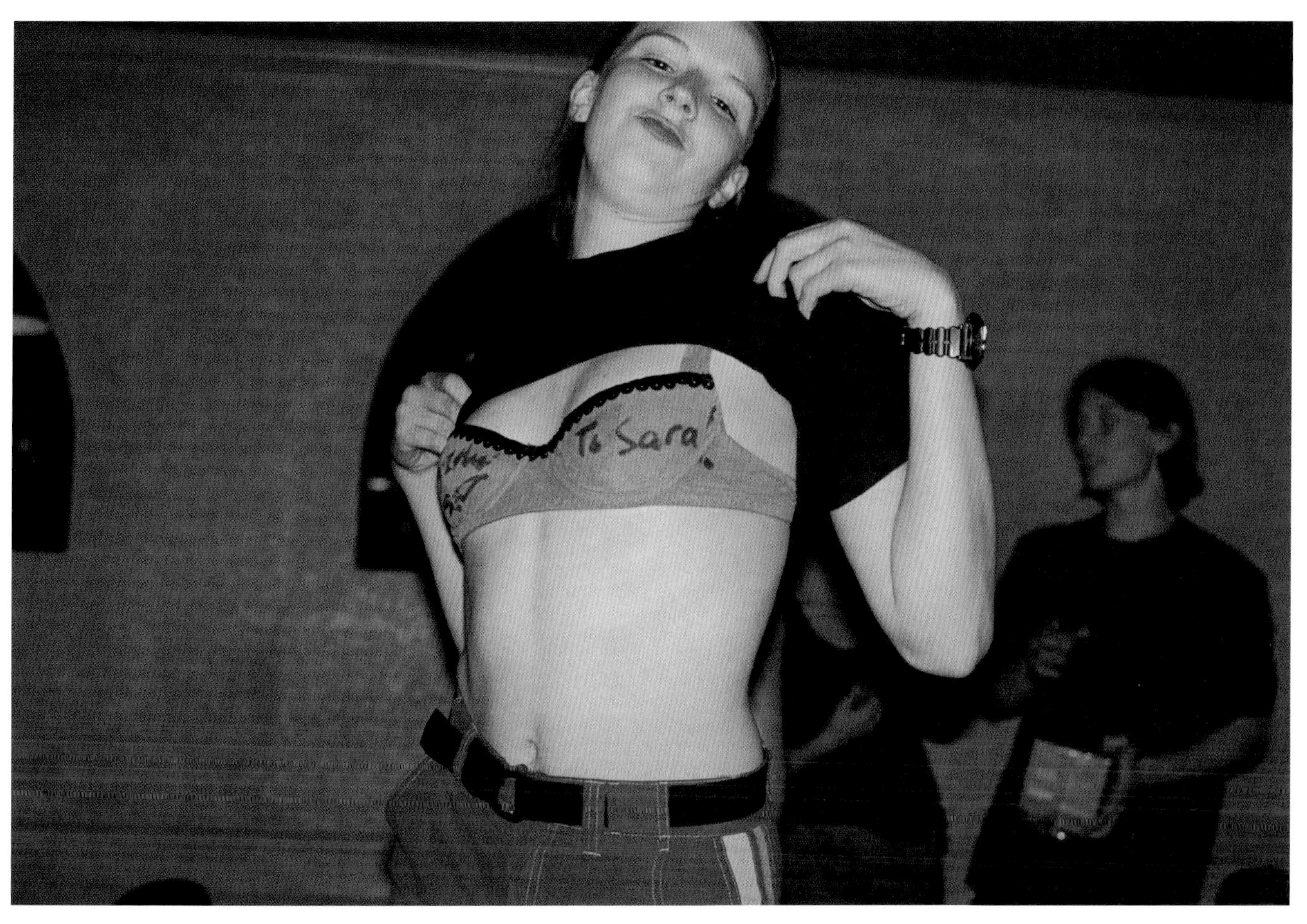

TC

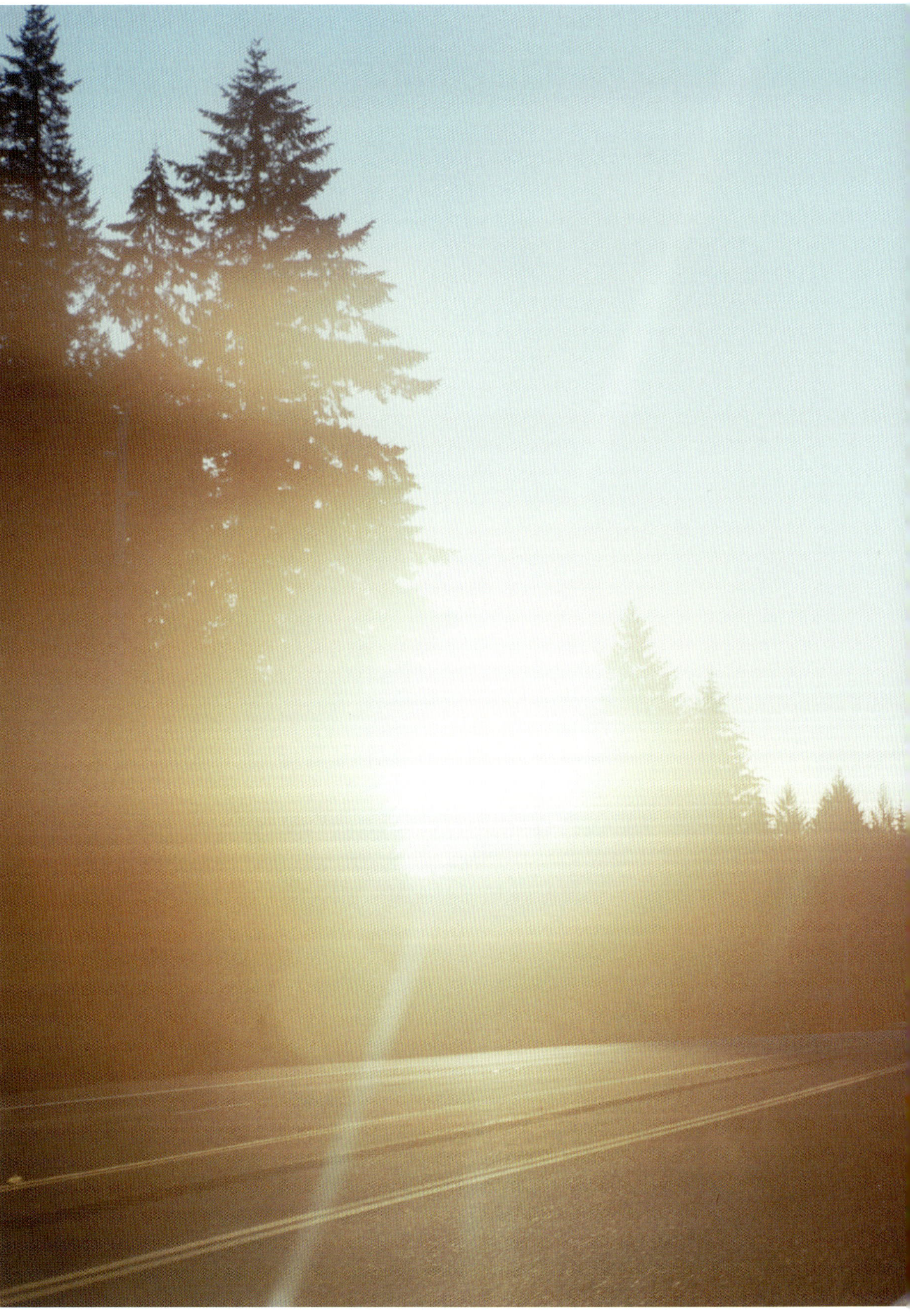

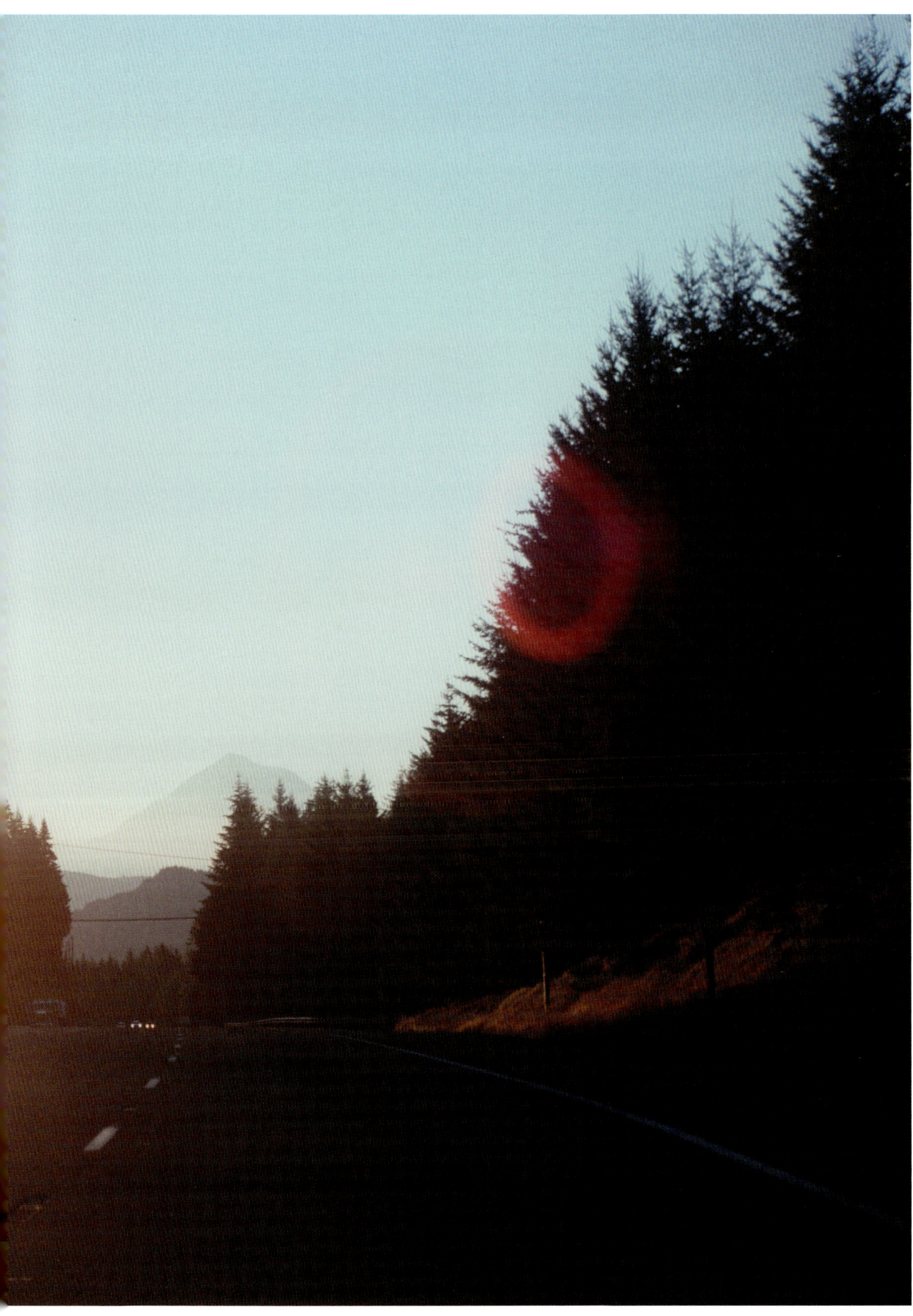

MB

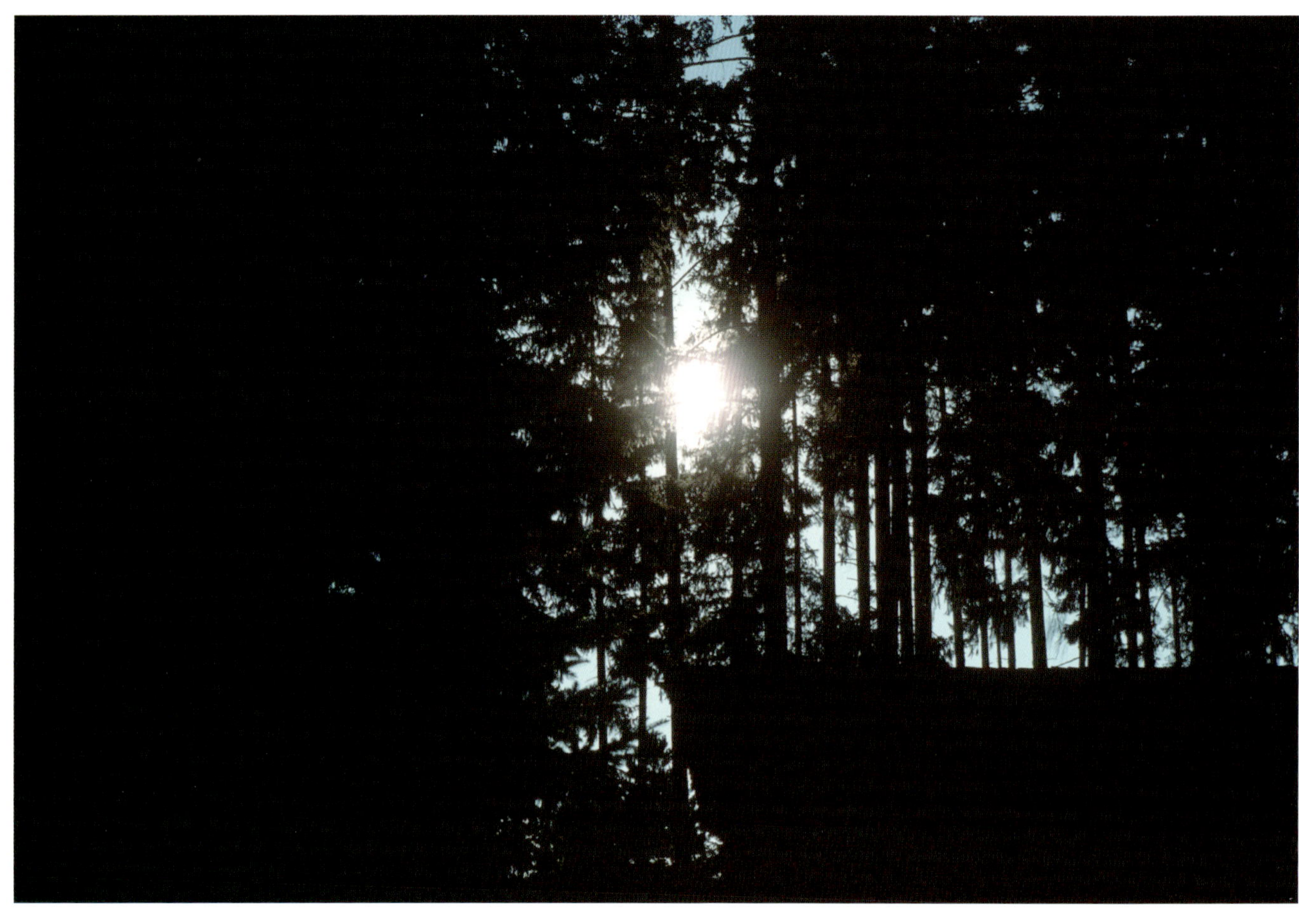

MB

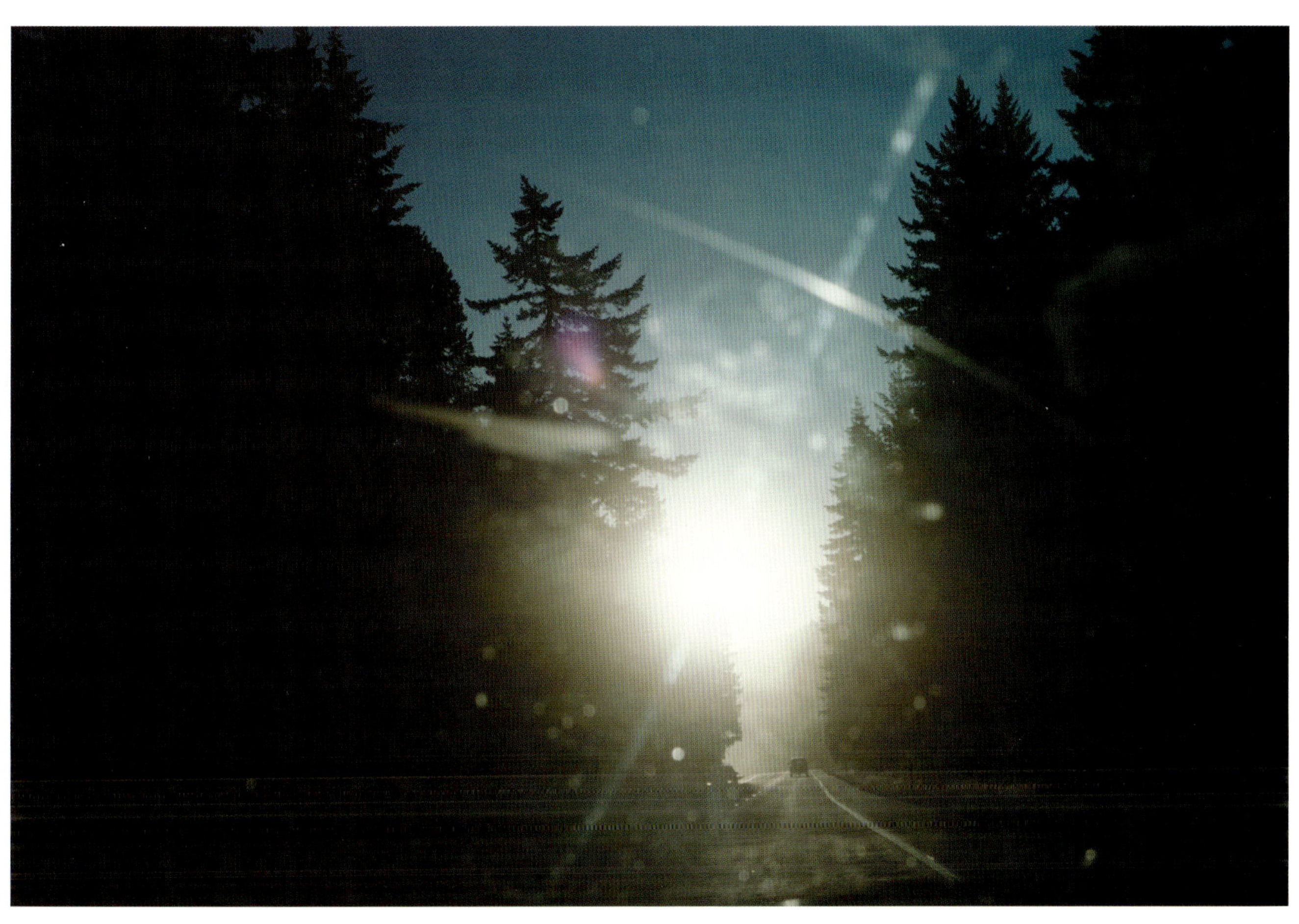

MB

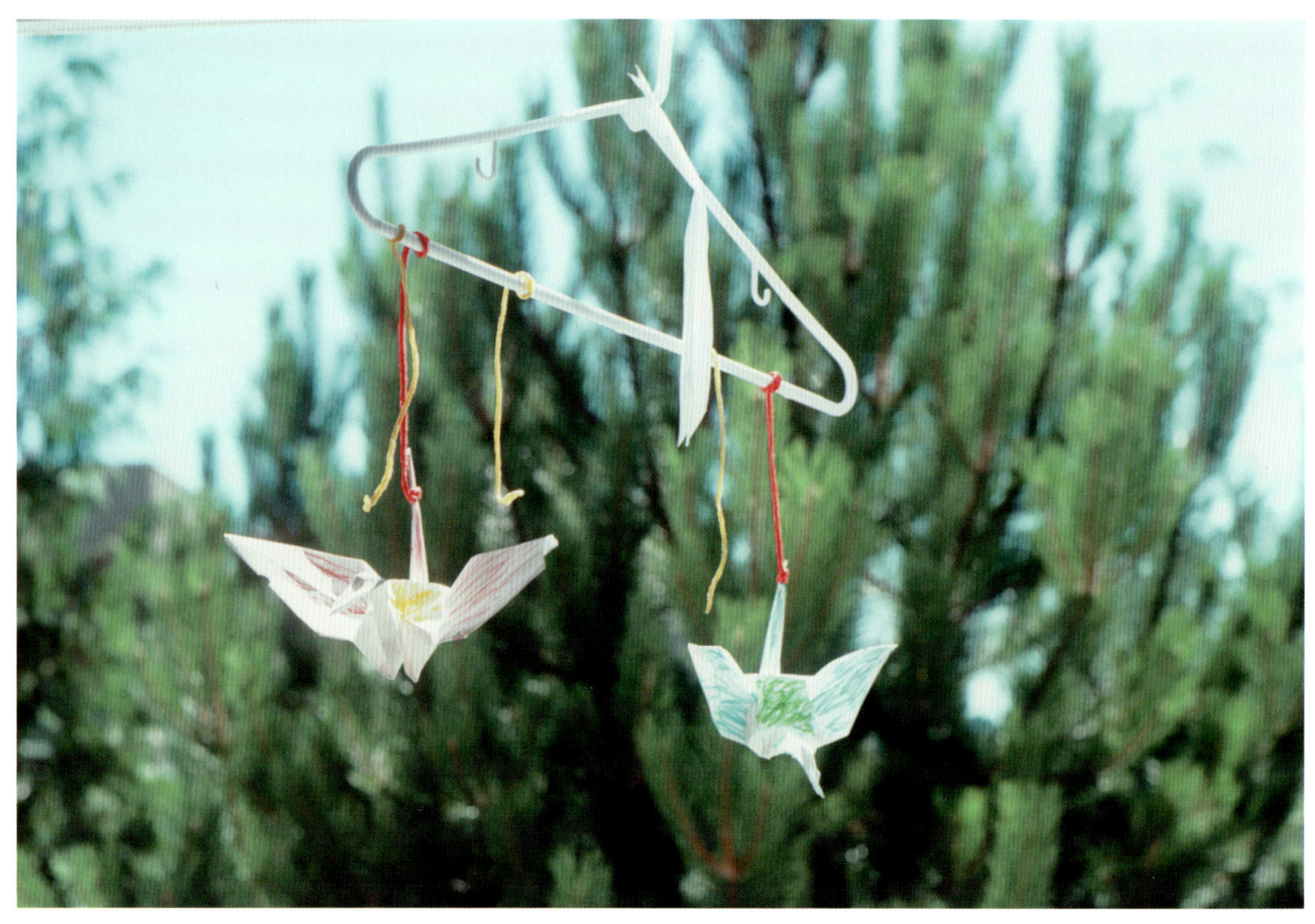

MB

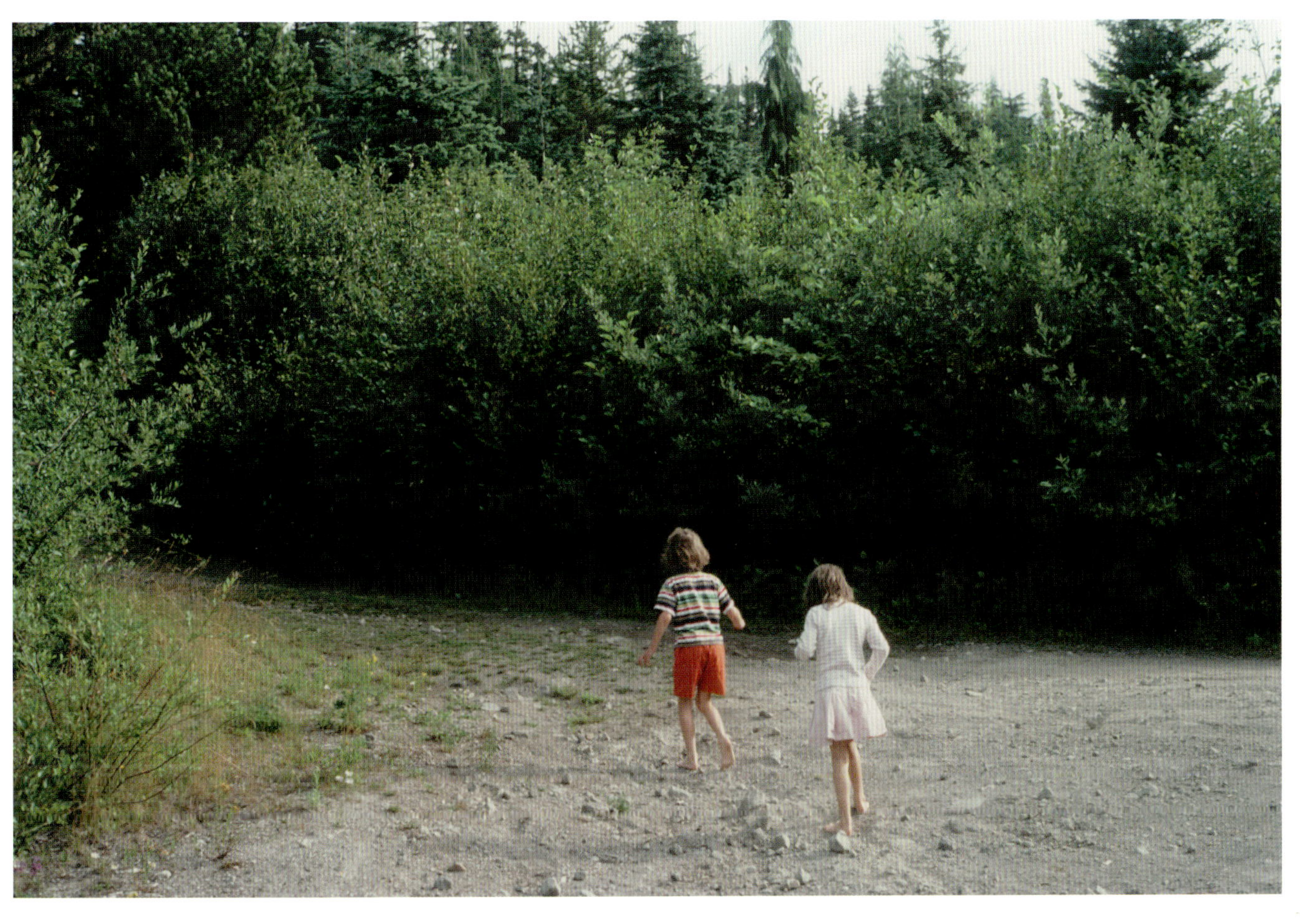

MB

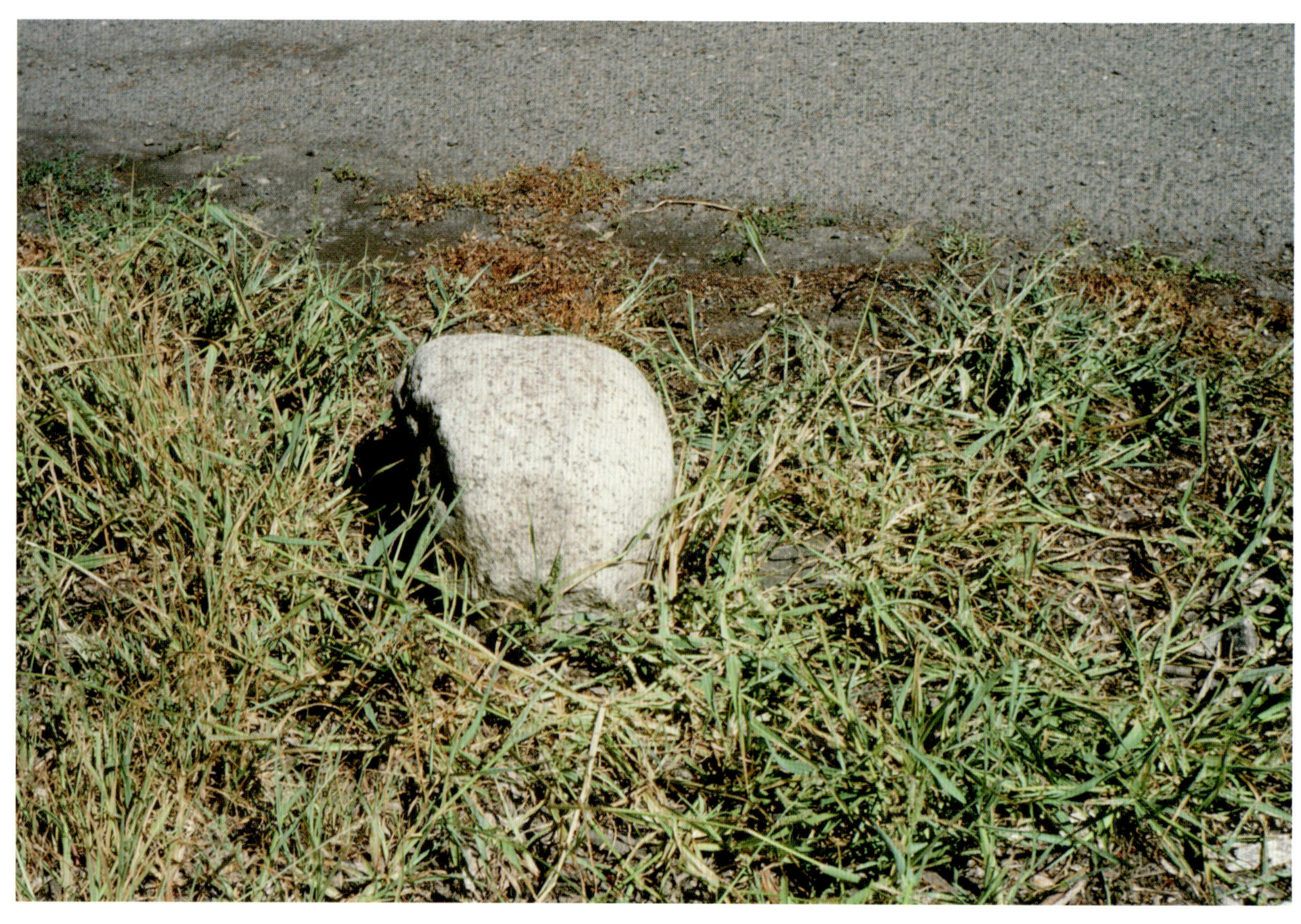

MB

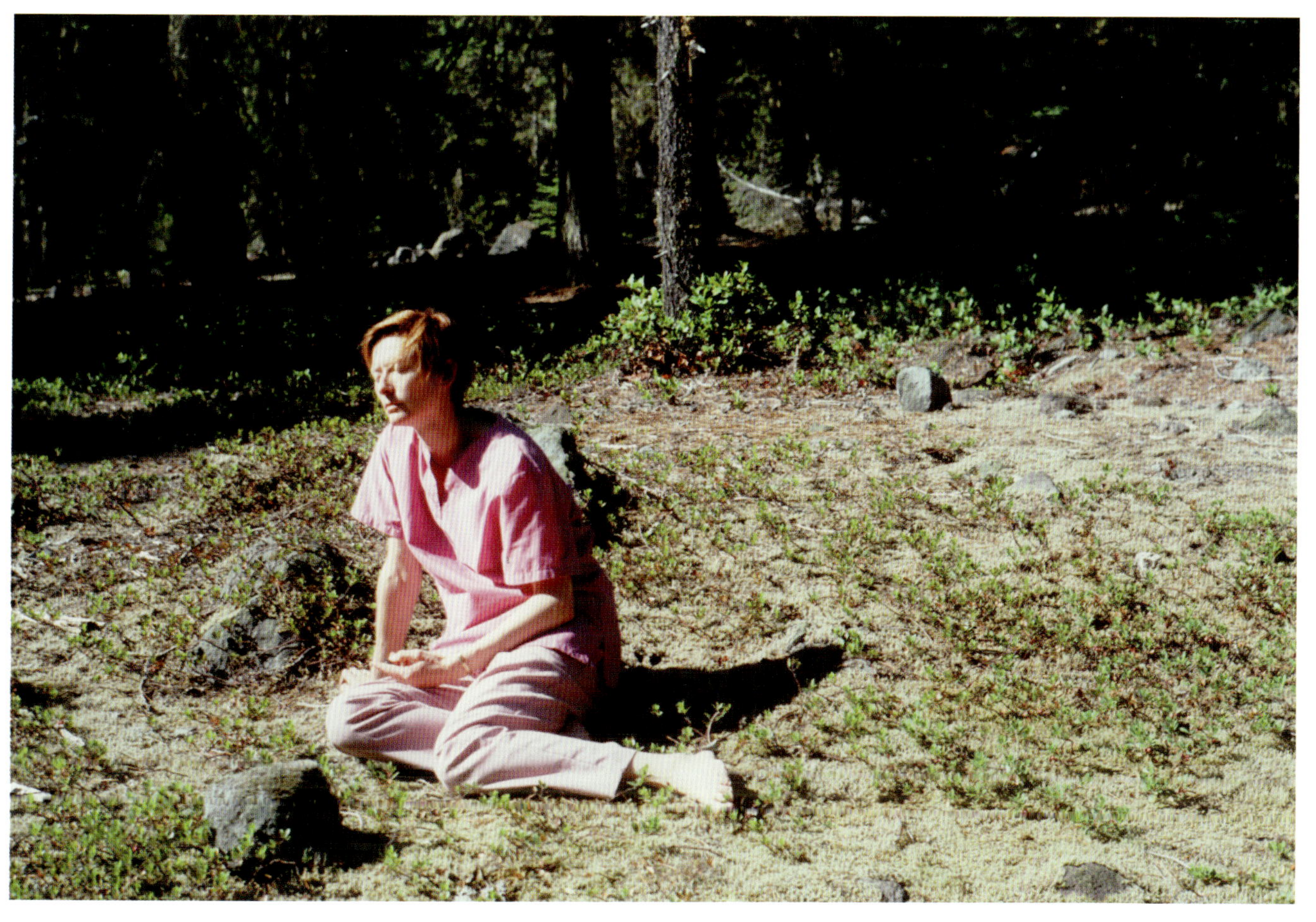

MB

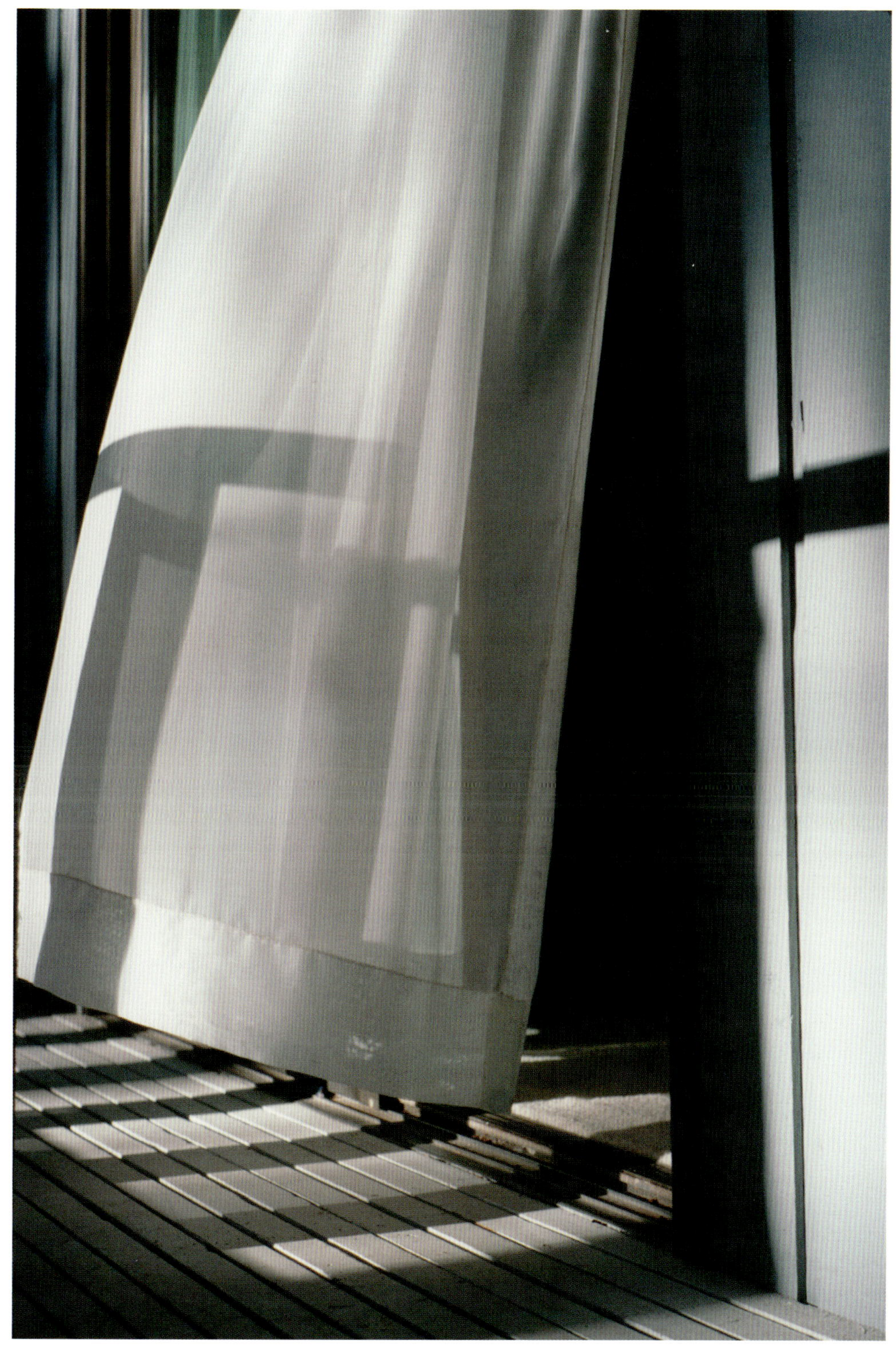

MB

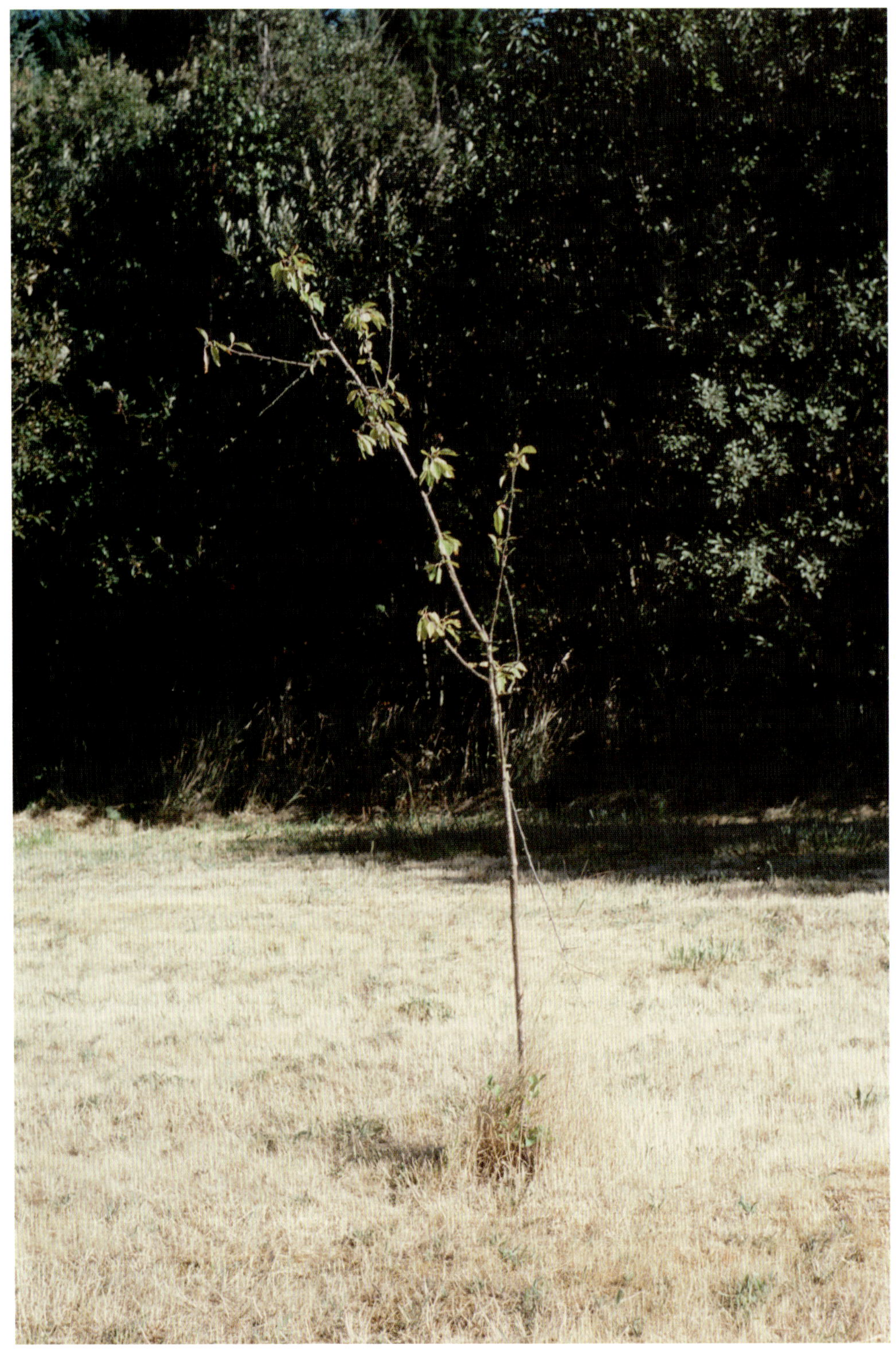

MB

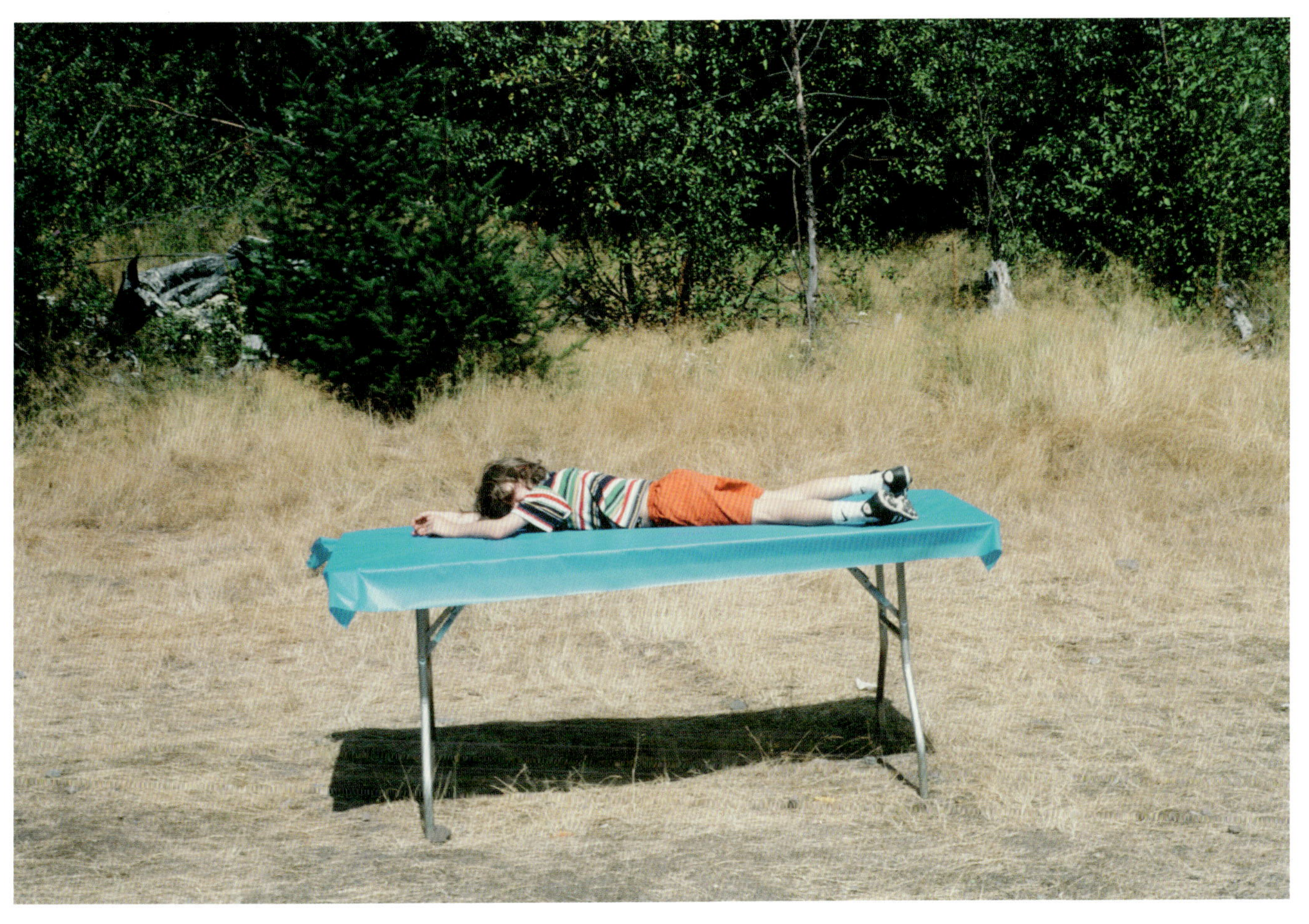

MB

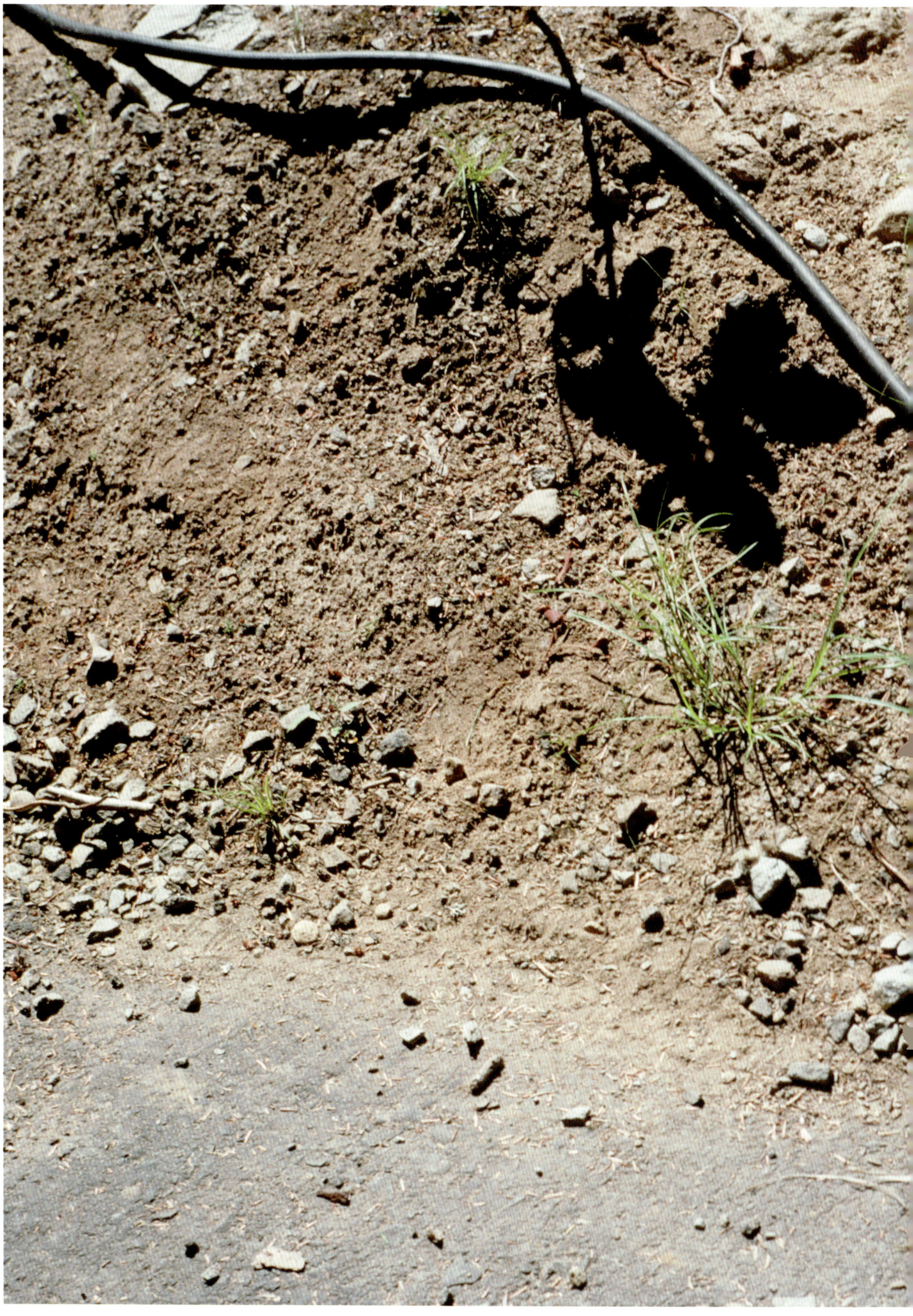

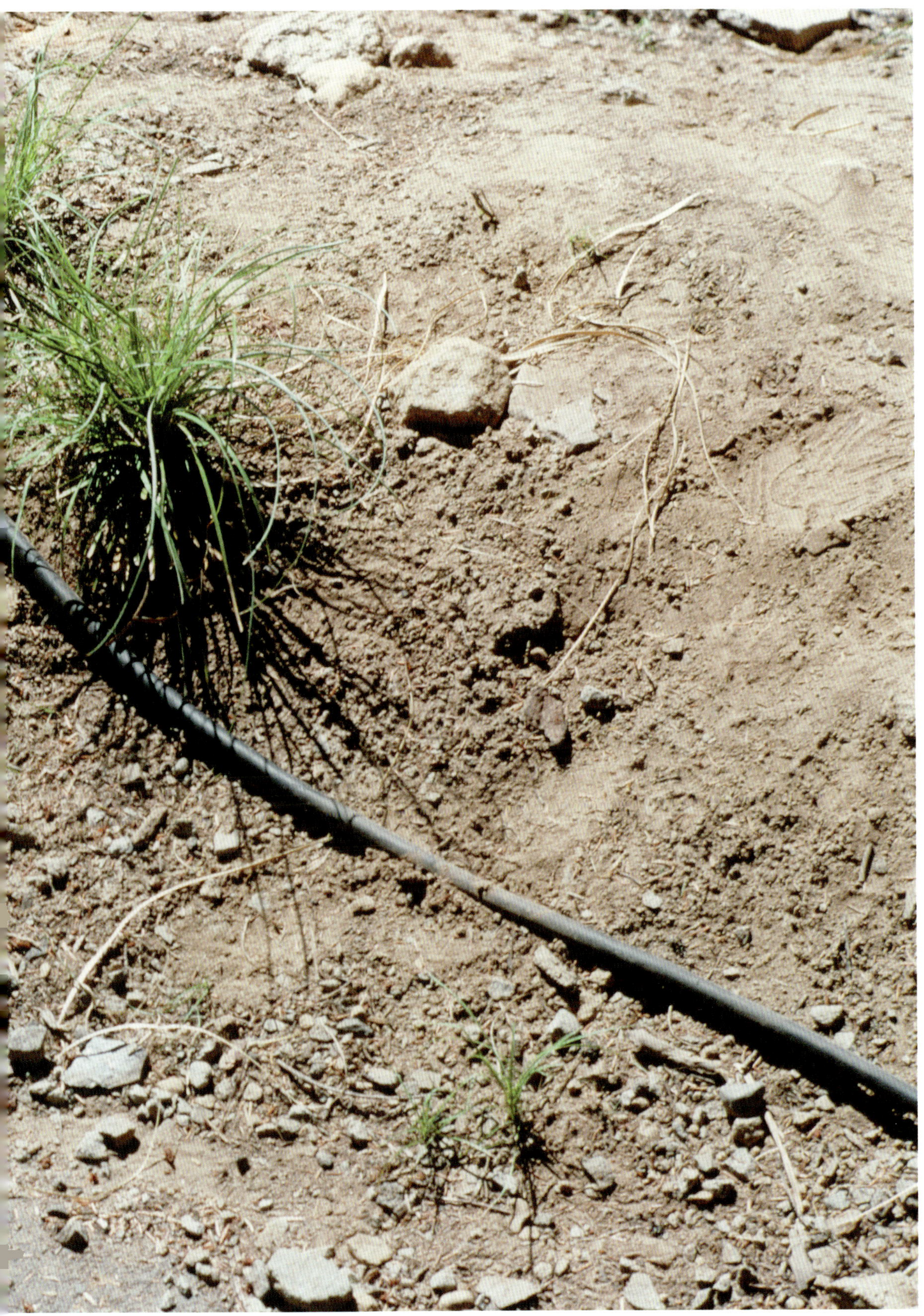

MB

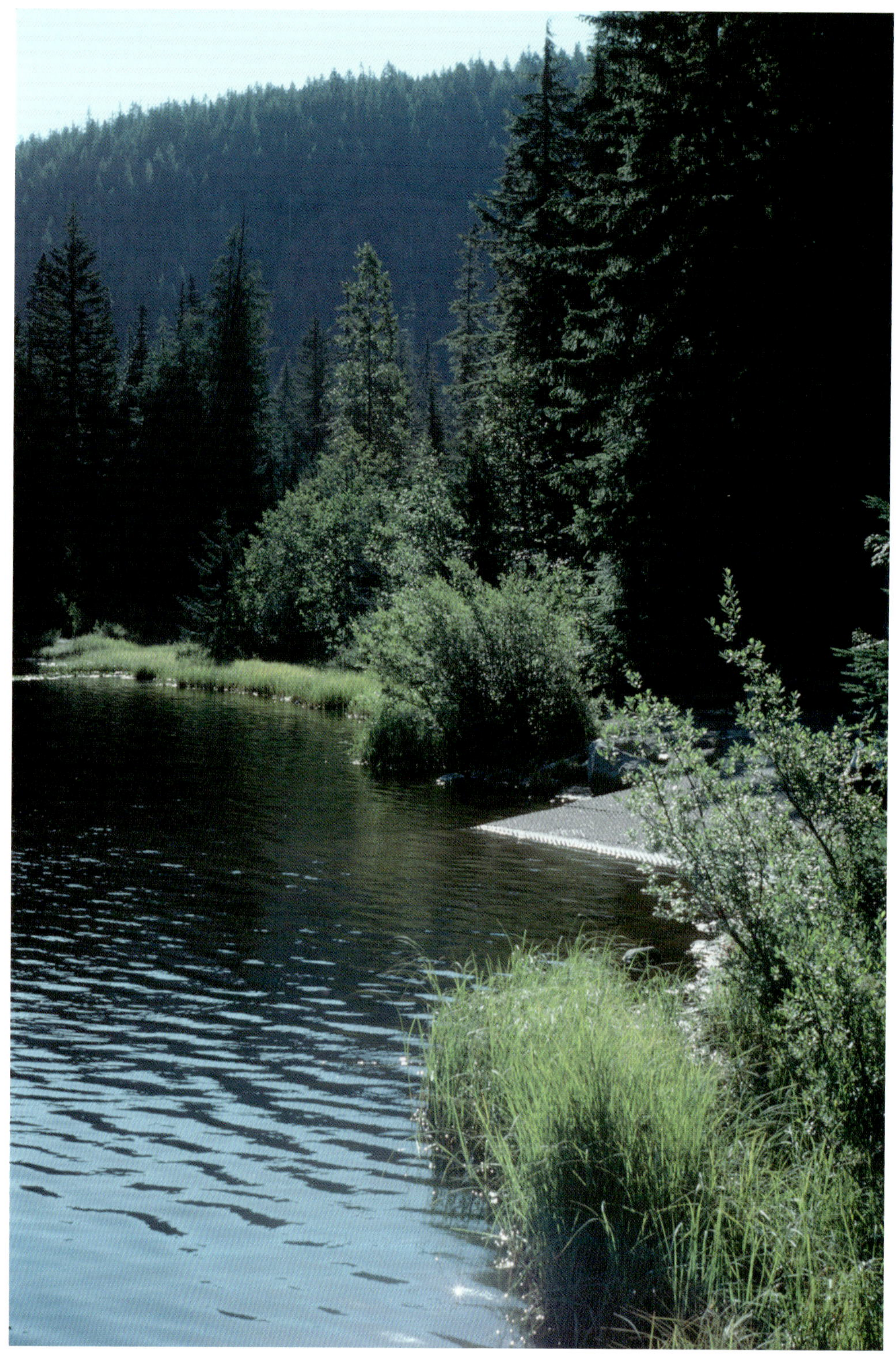

MB

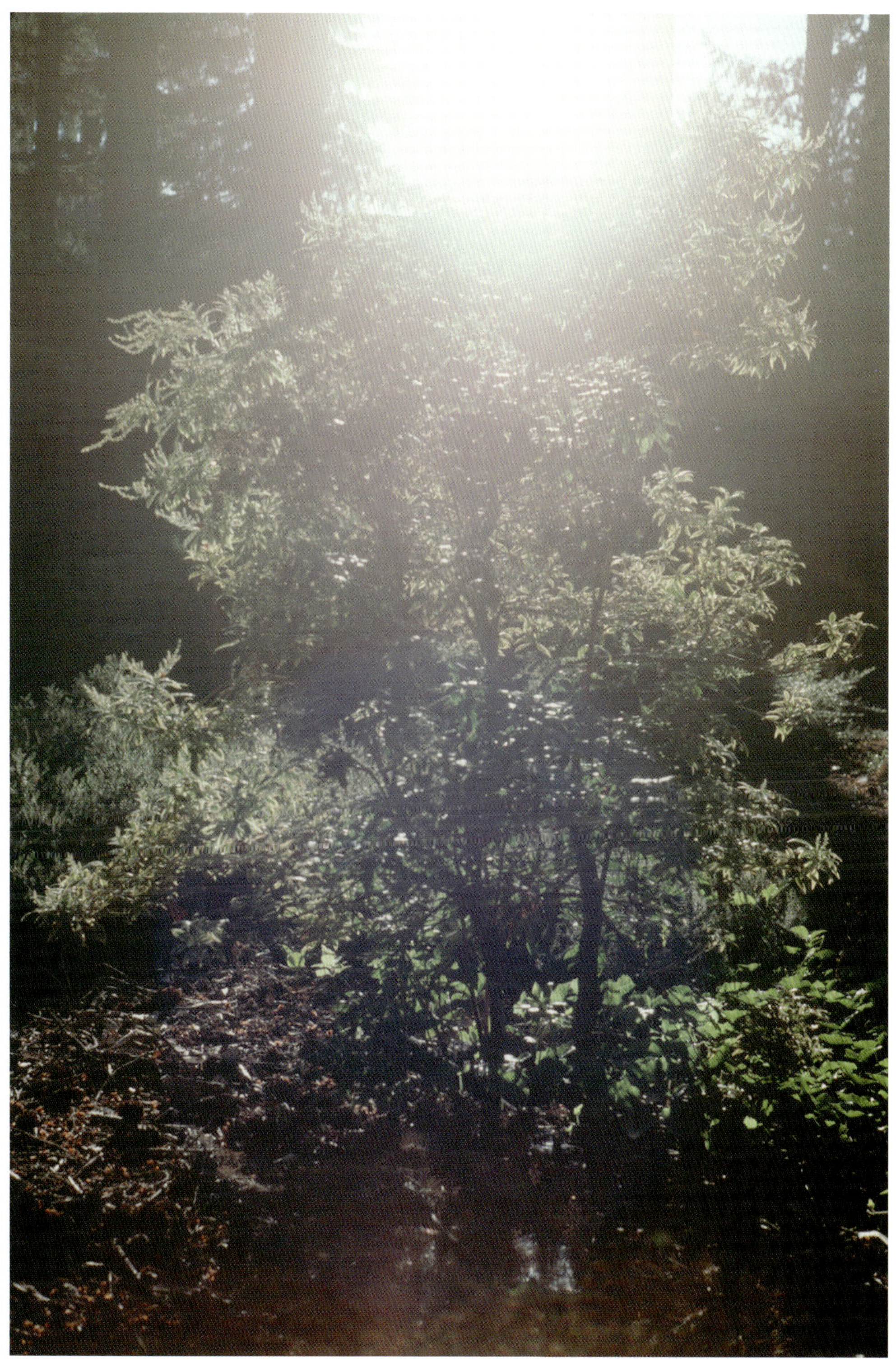

MB

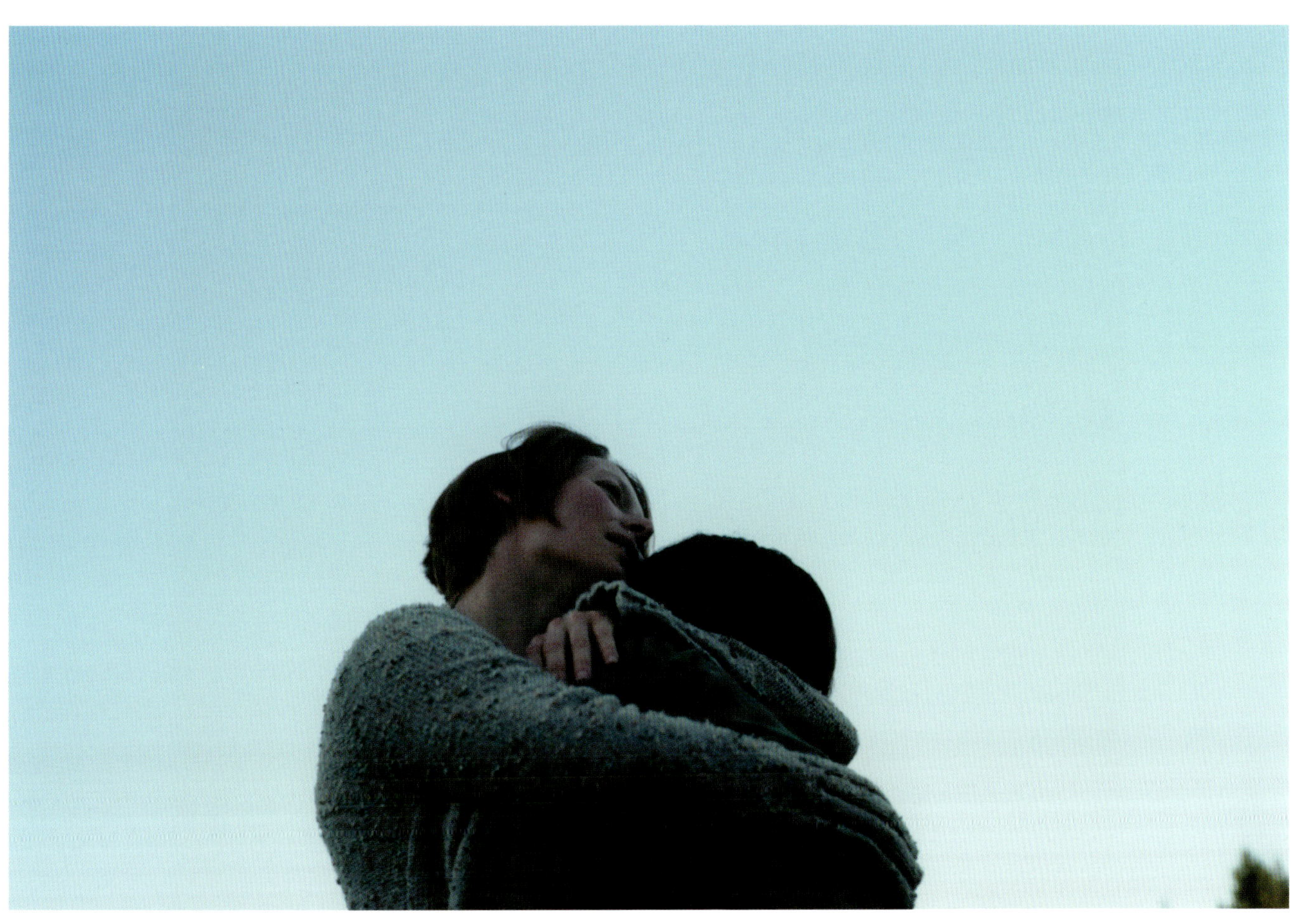

MB

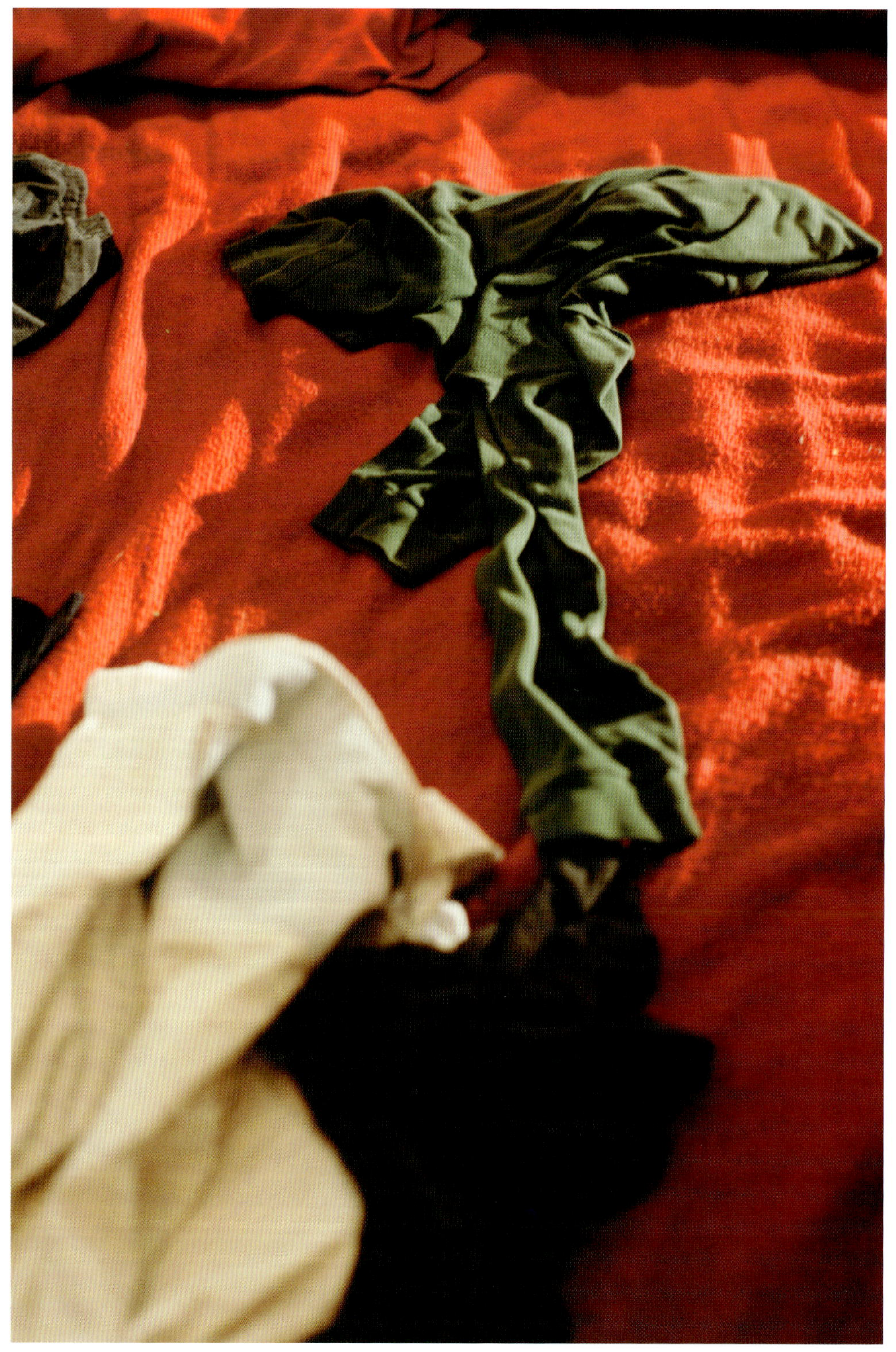

MB

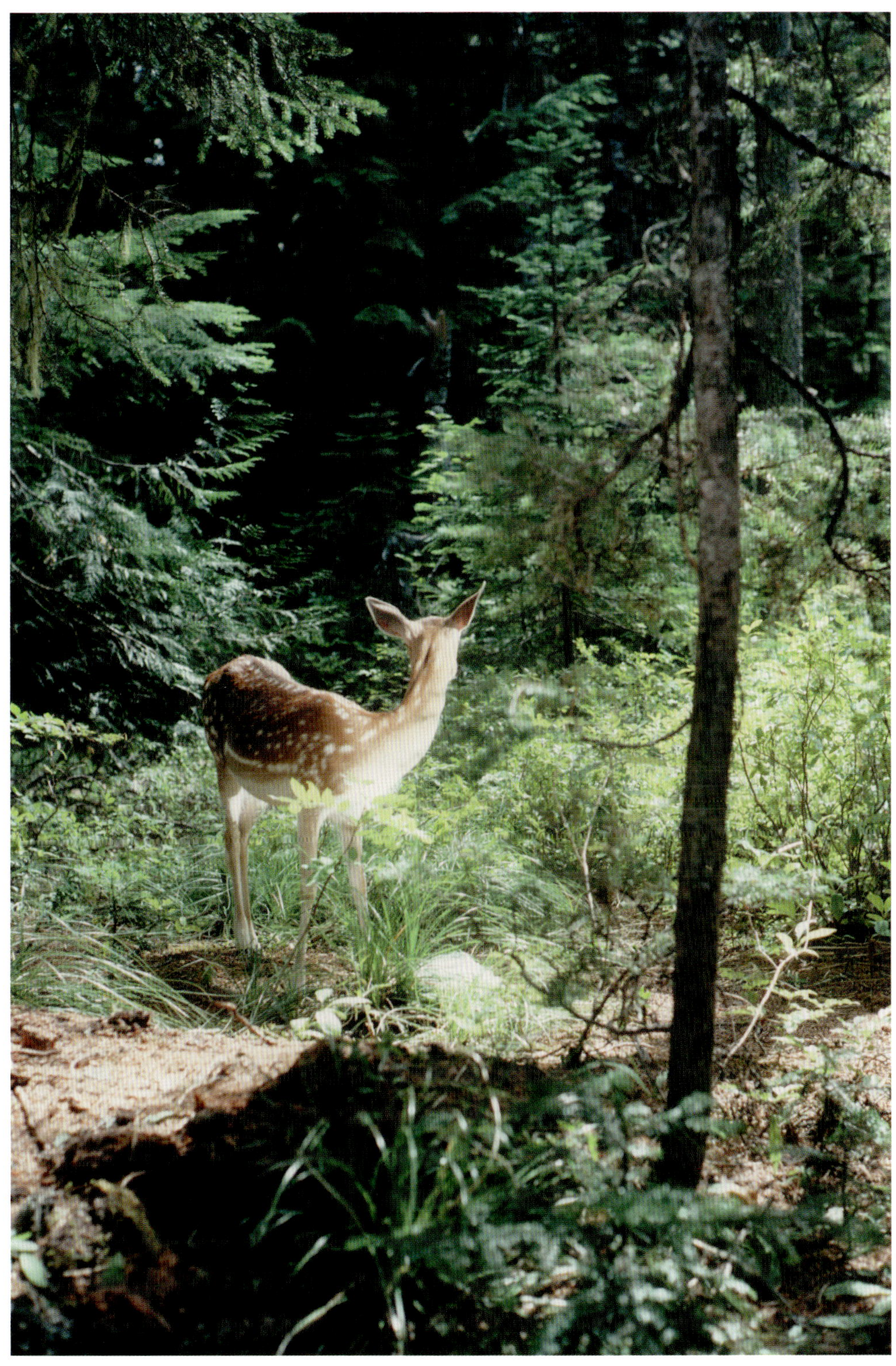

MB

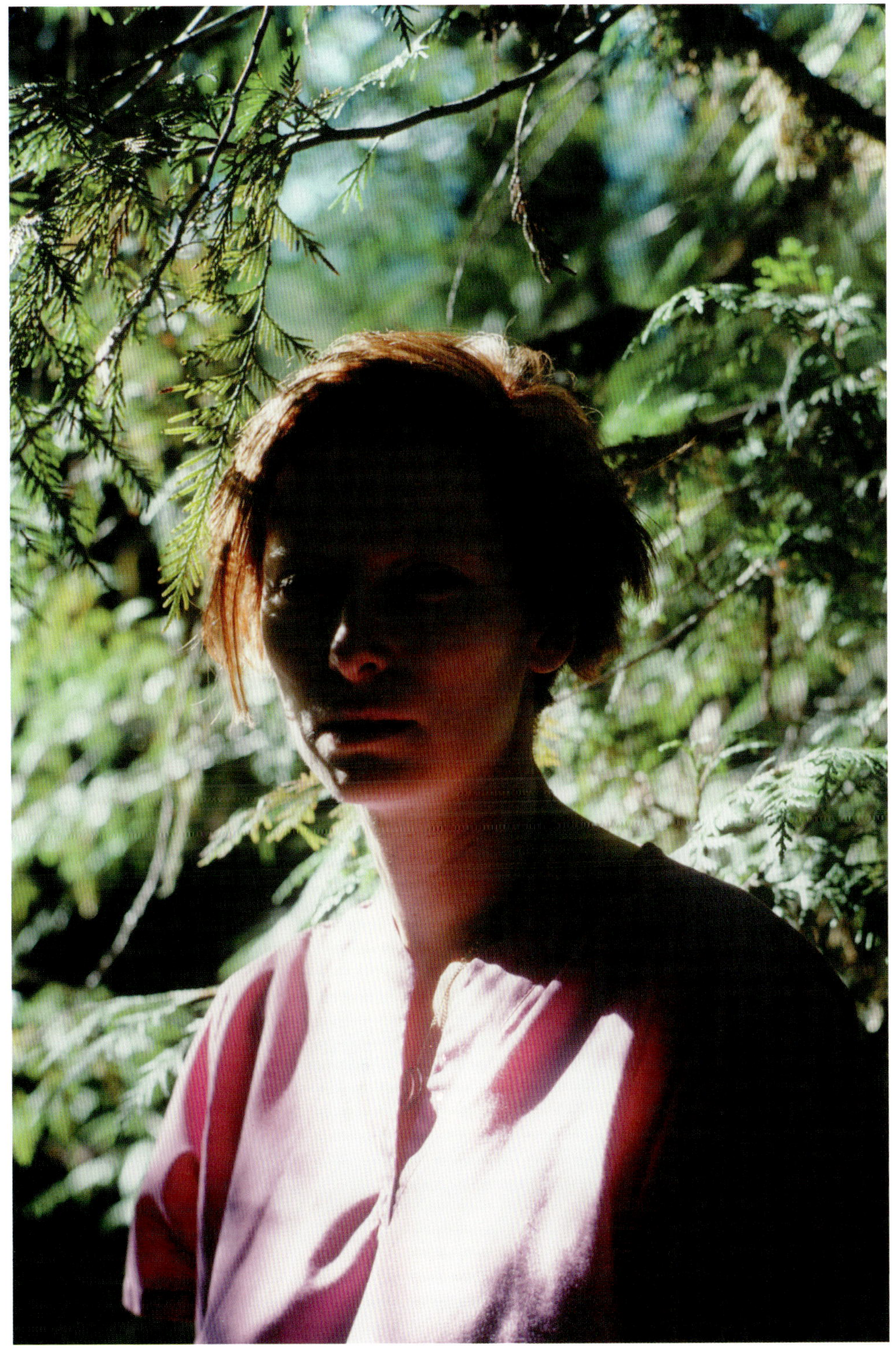

MB

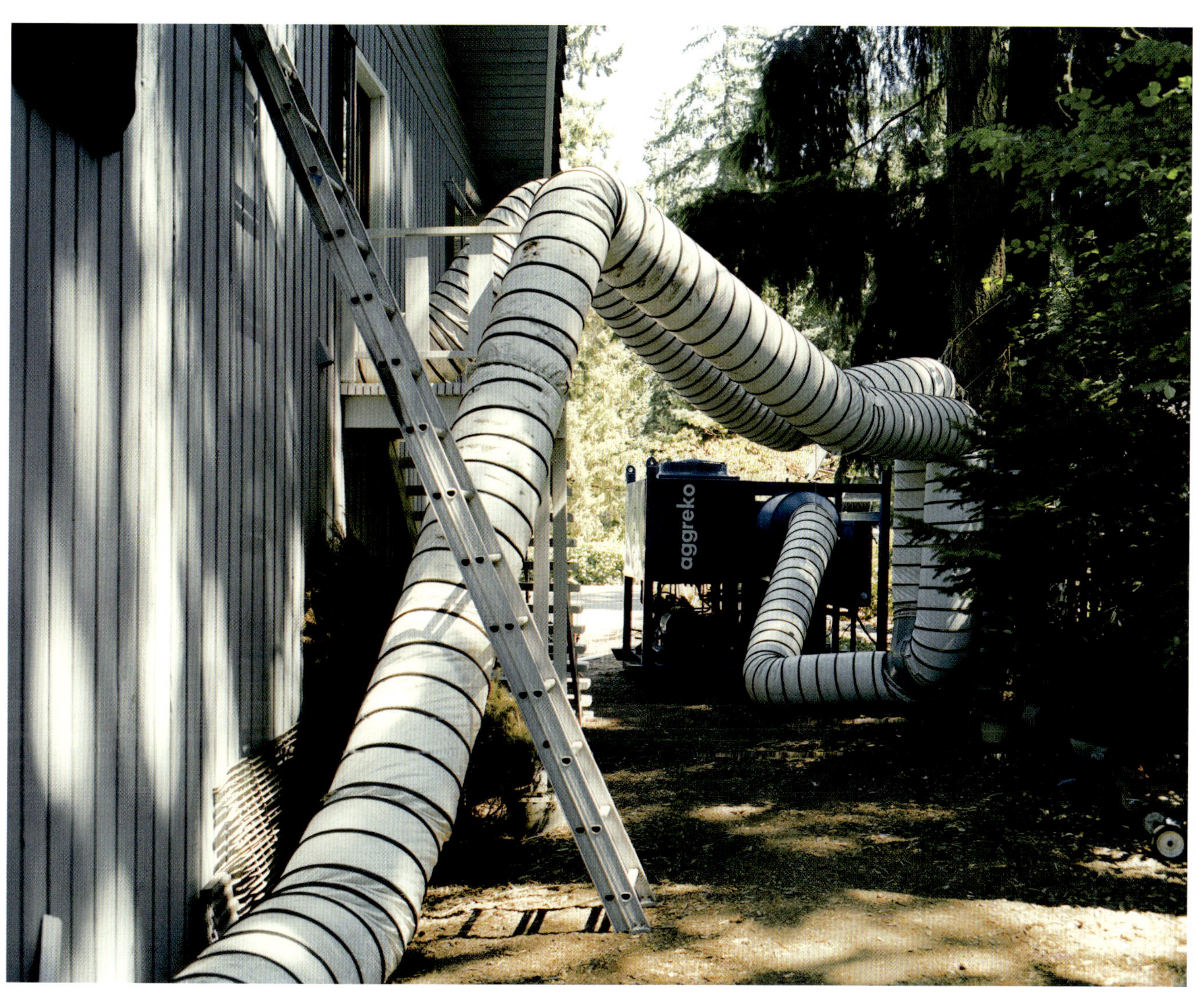

TC

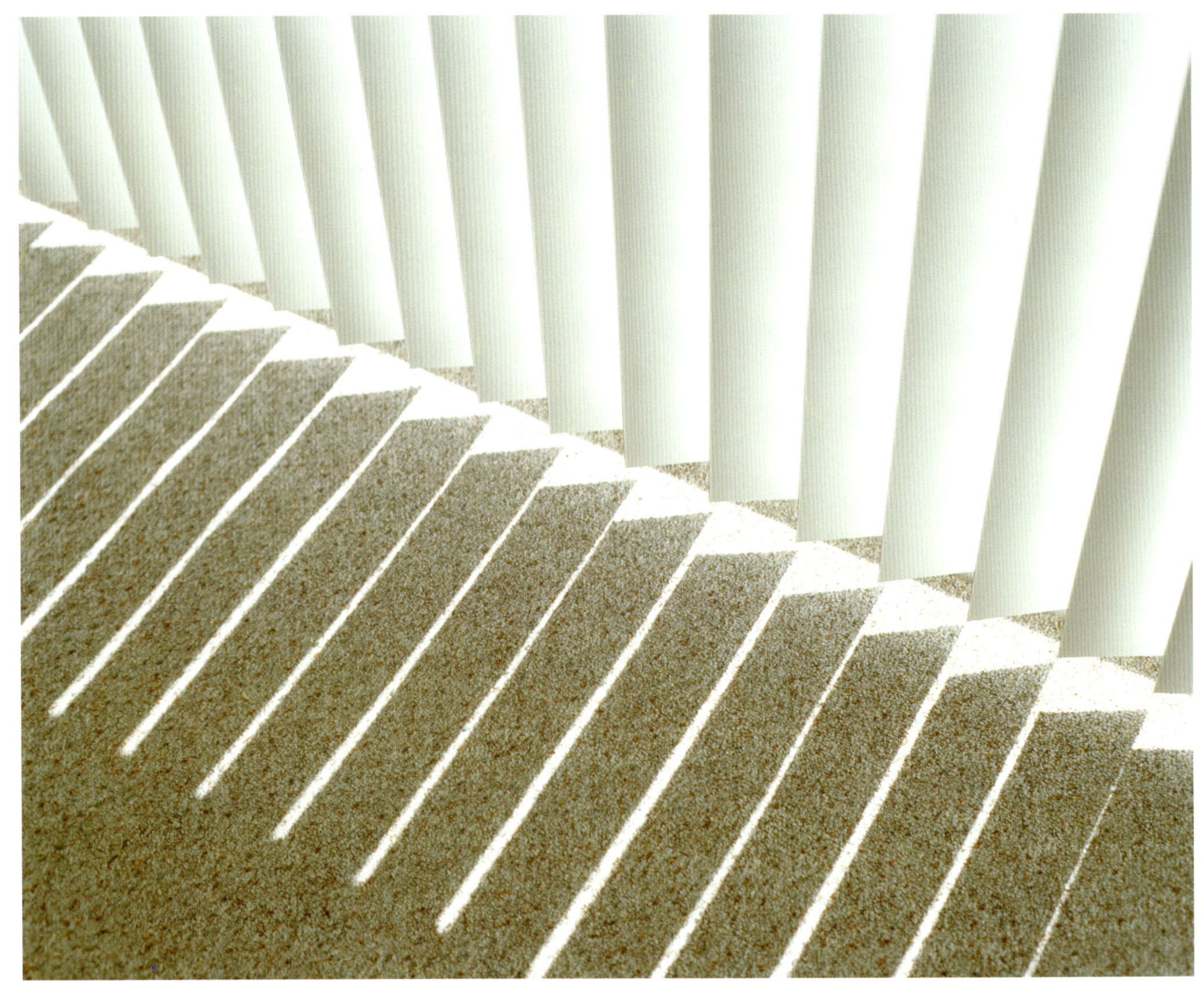

TC

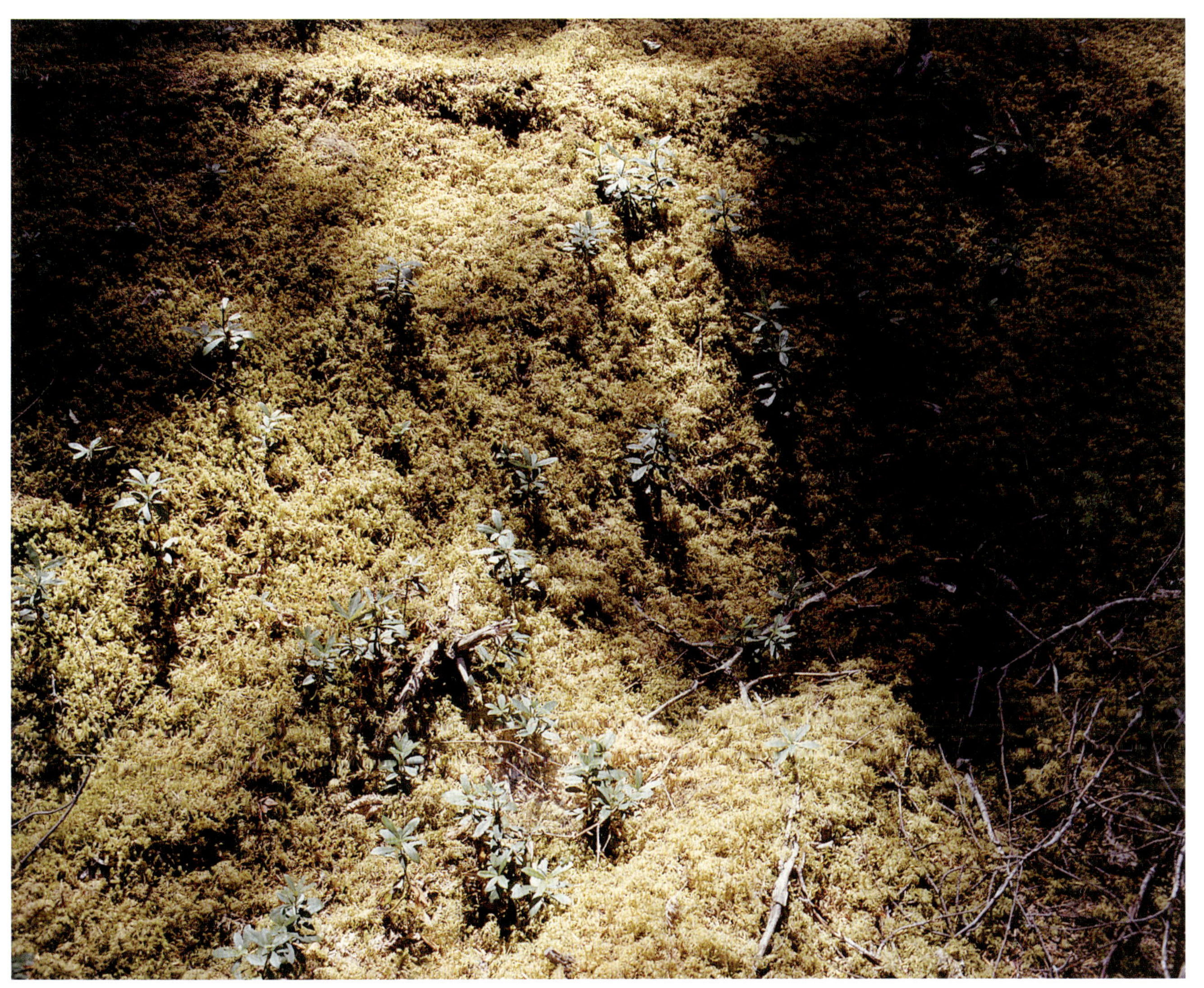

TC

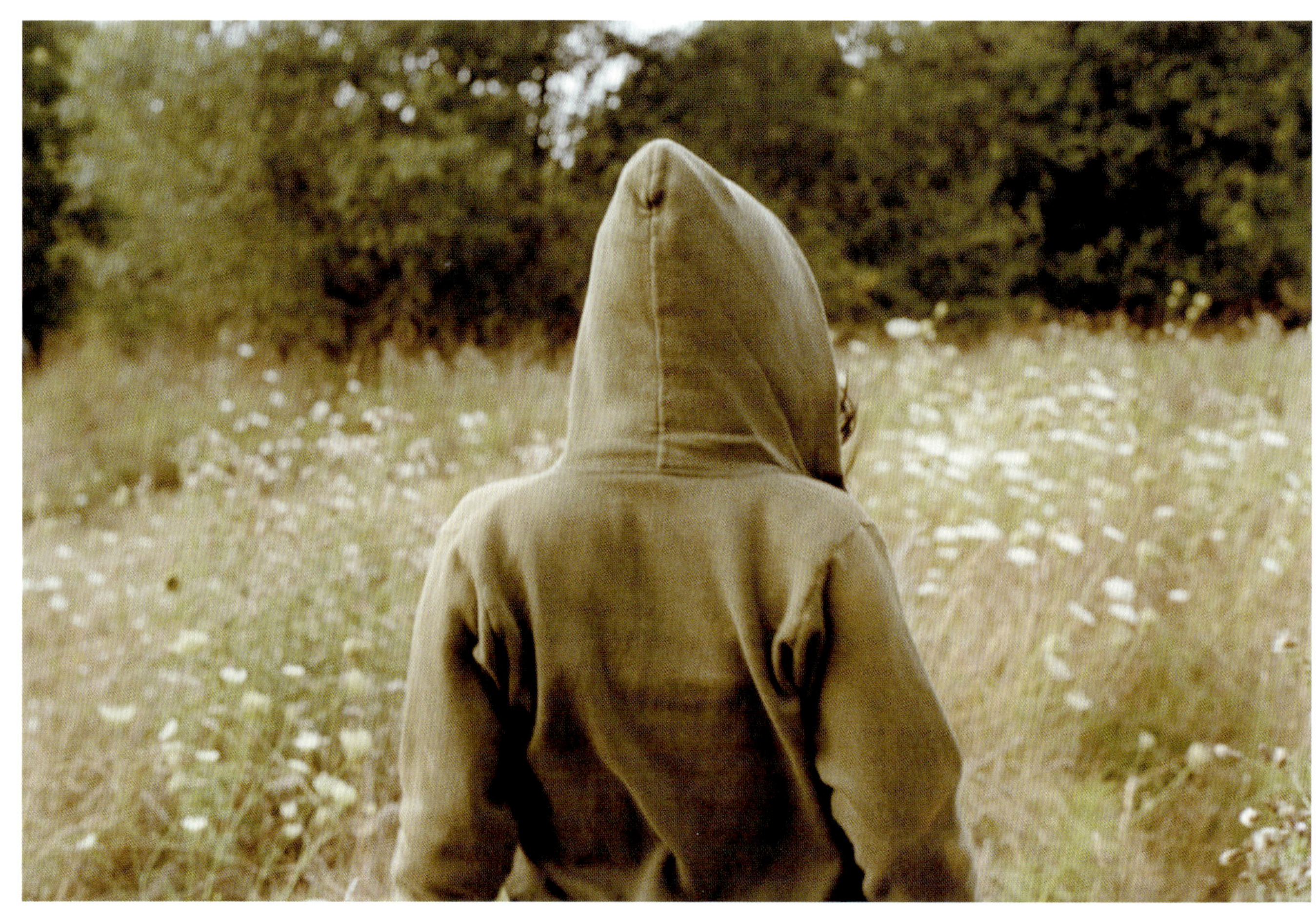

TC

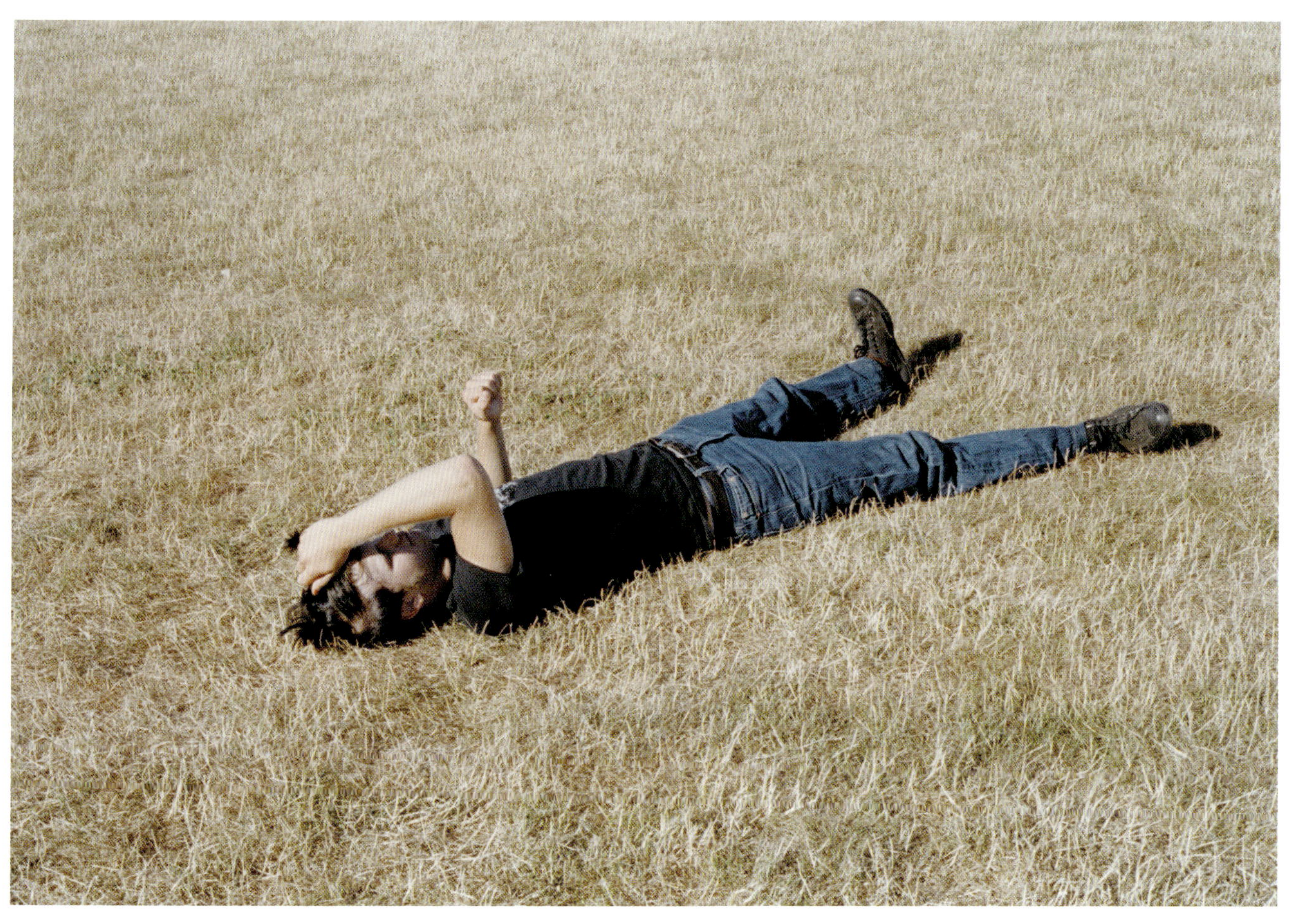

TC

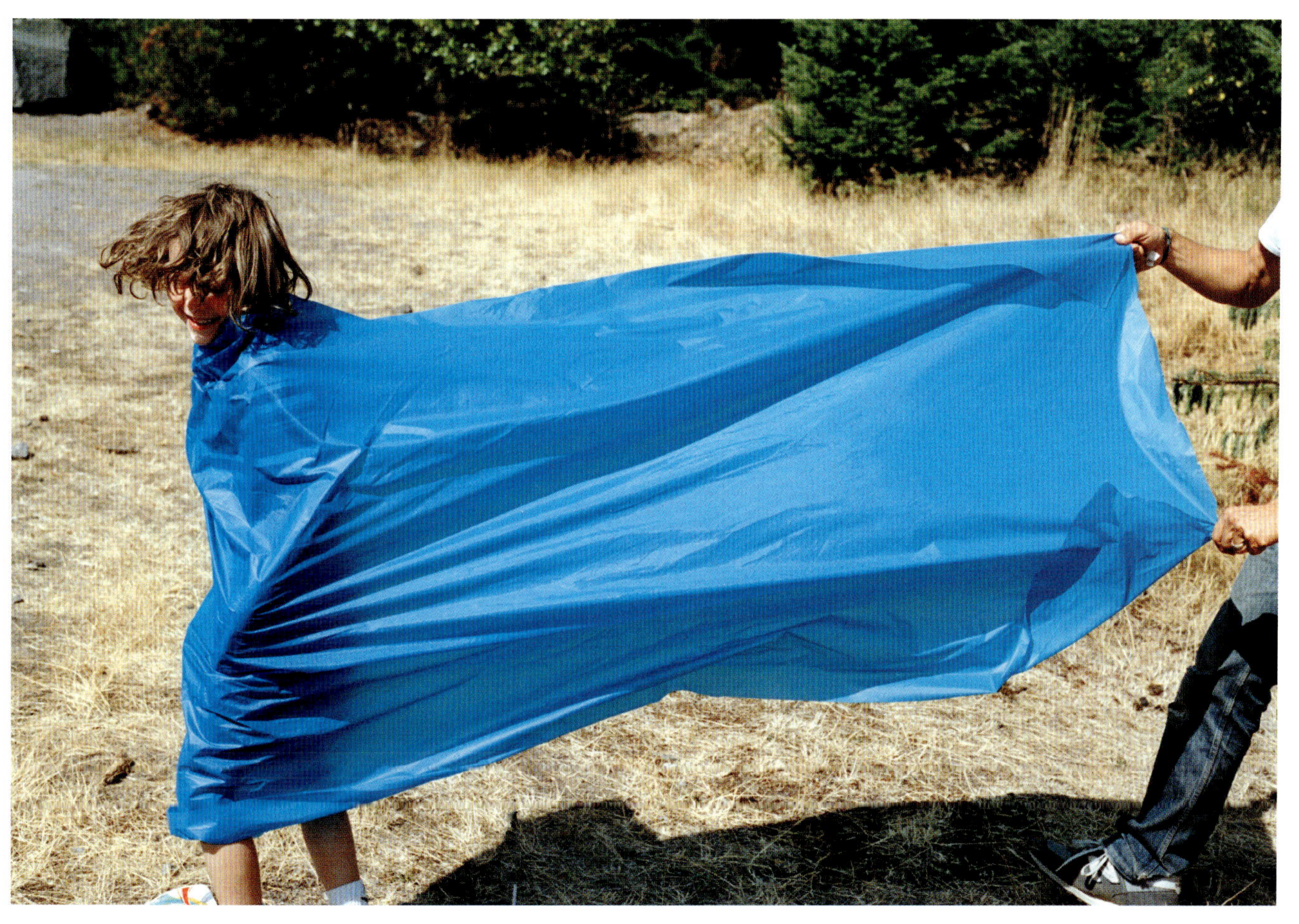

TC

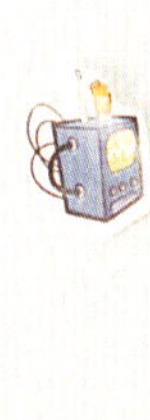
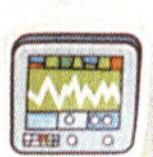

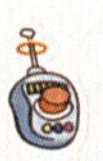
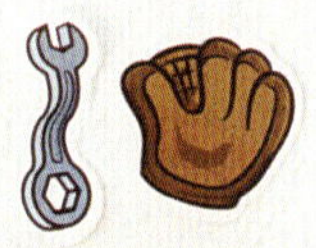
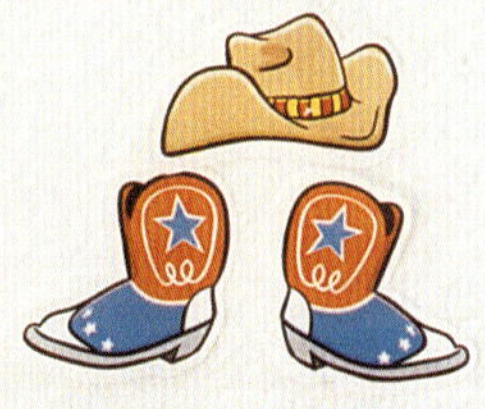

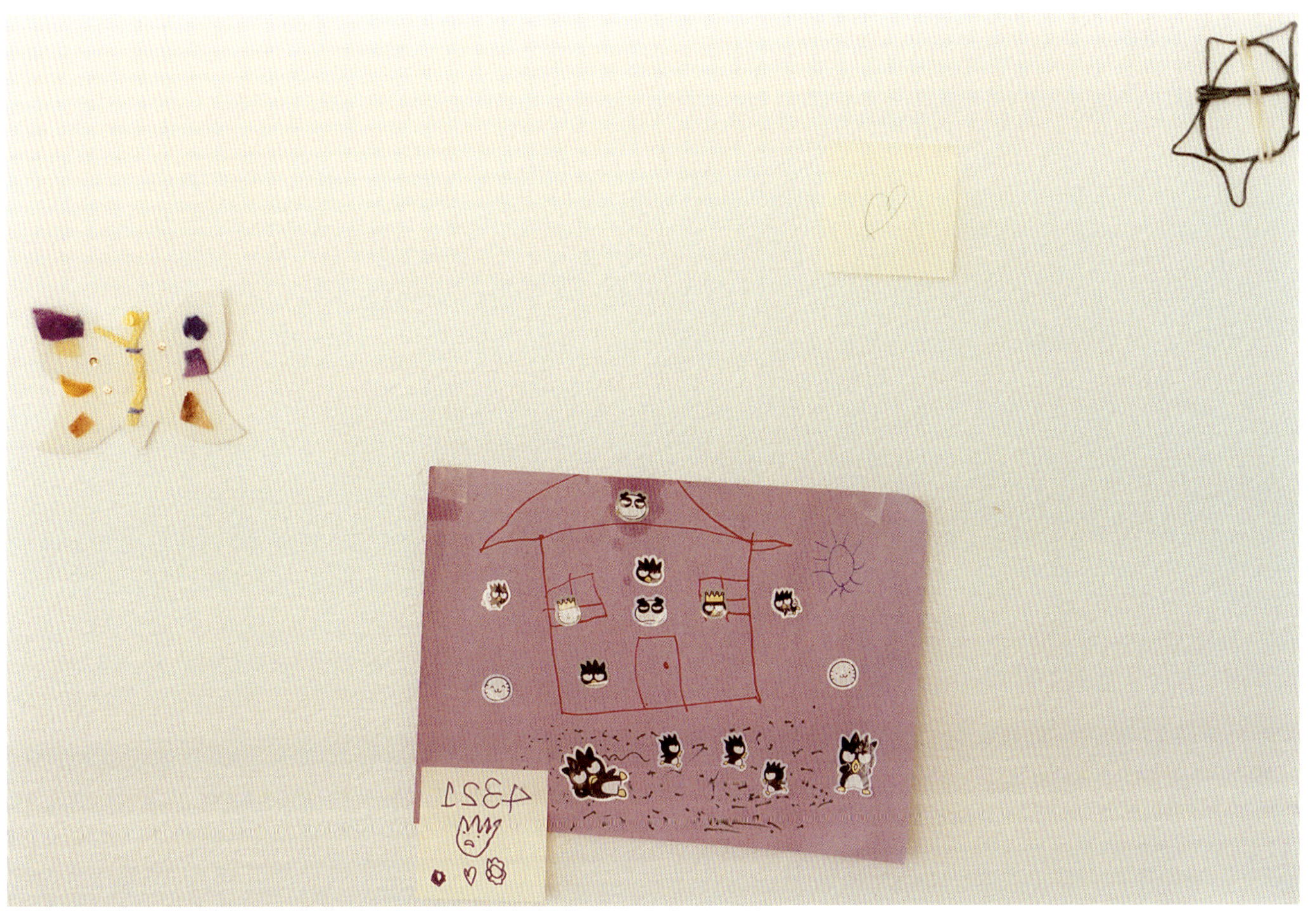

TC

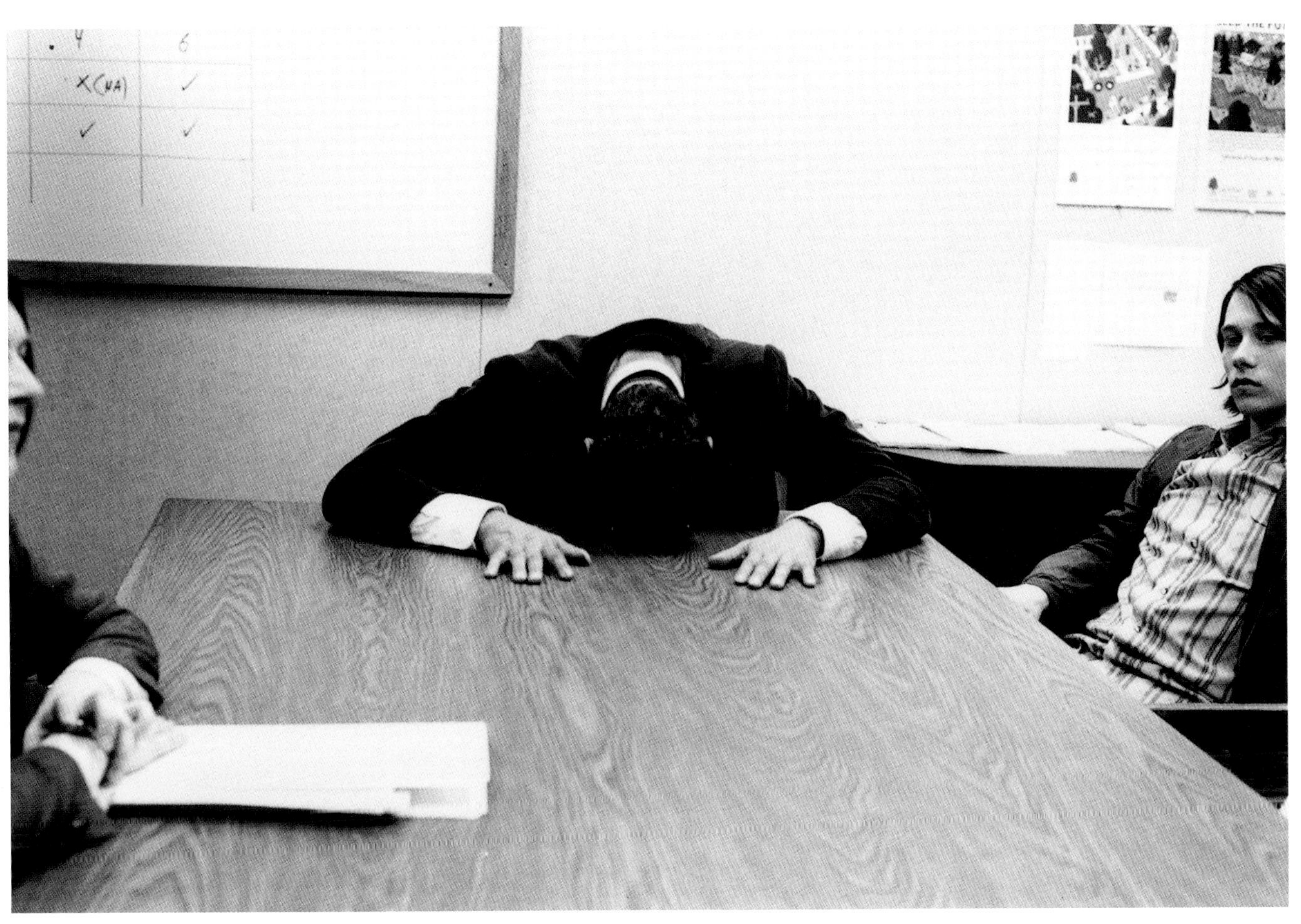

ET

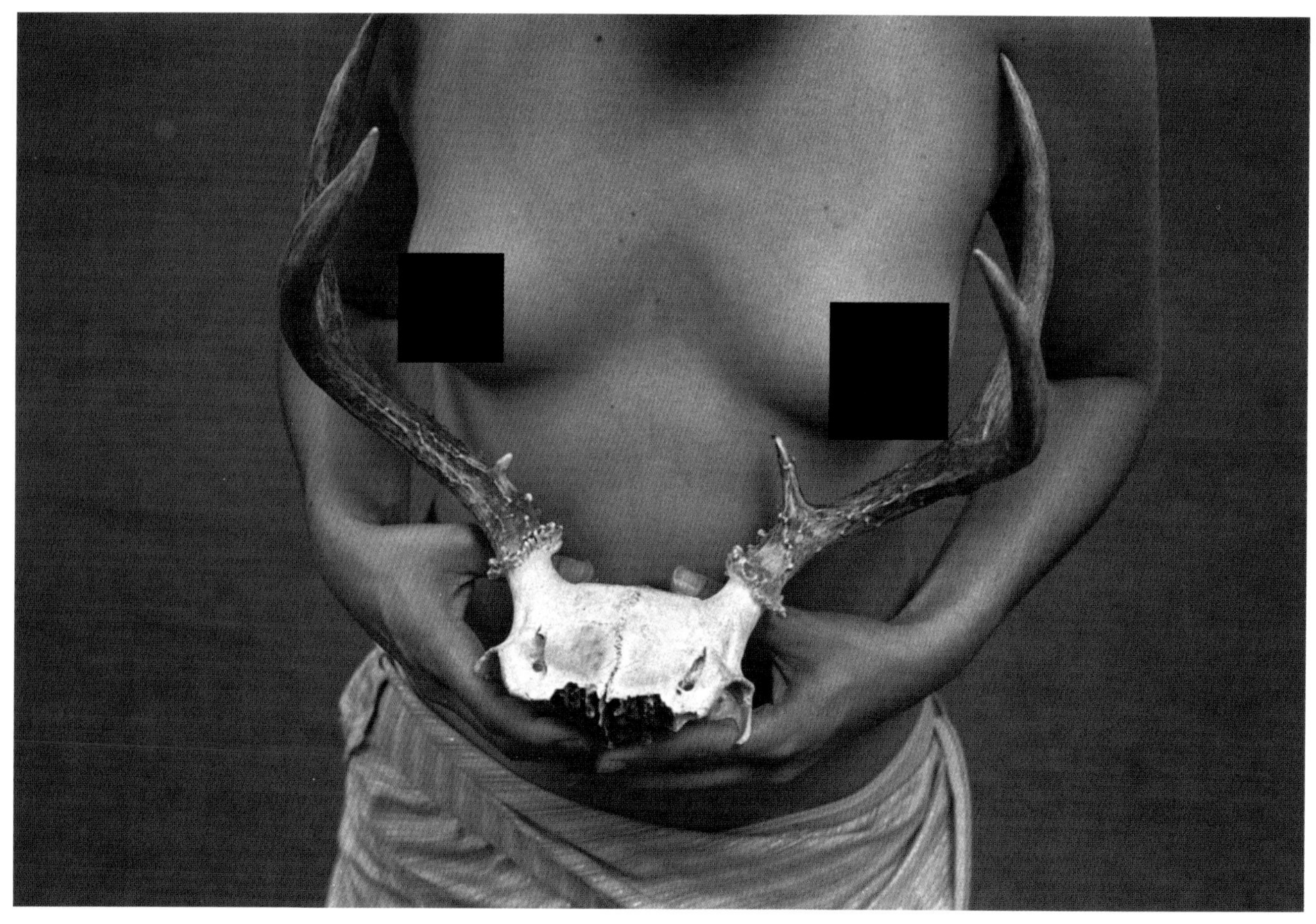

ET

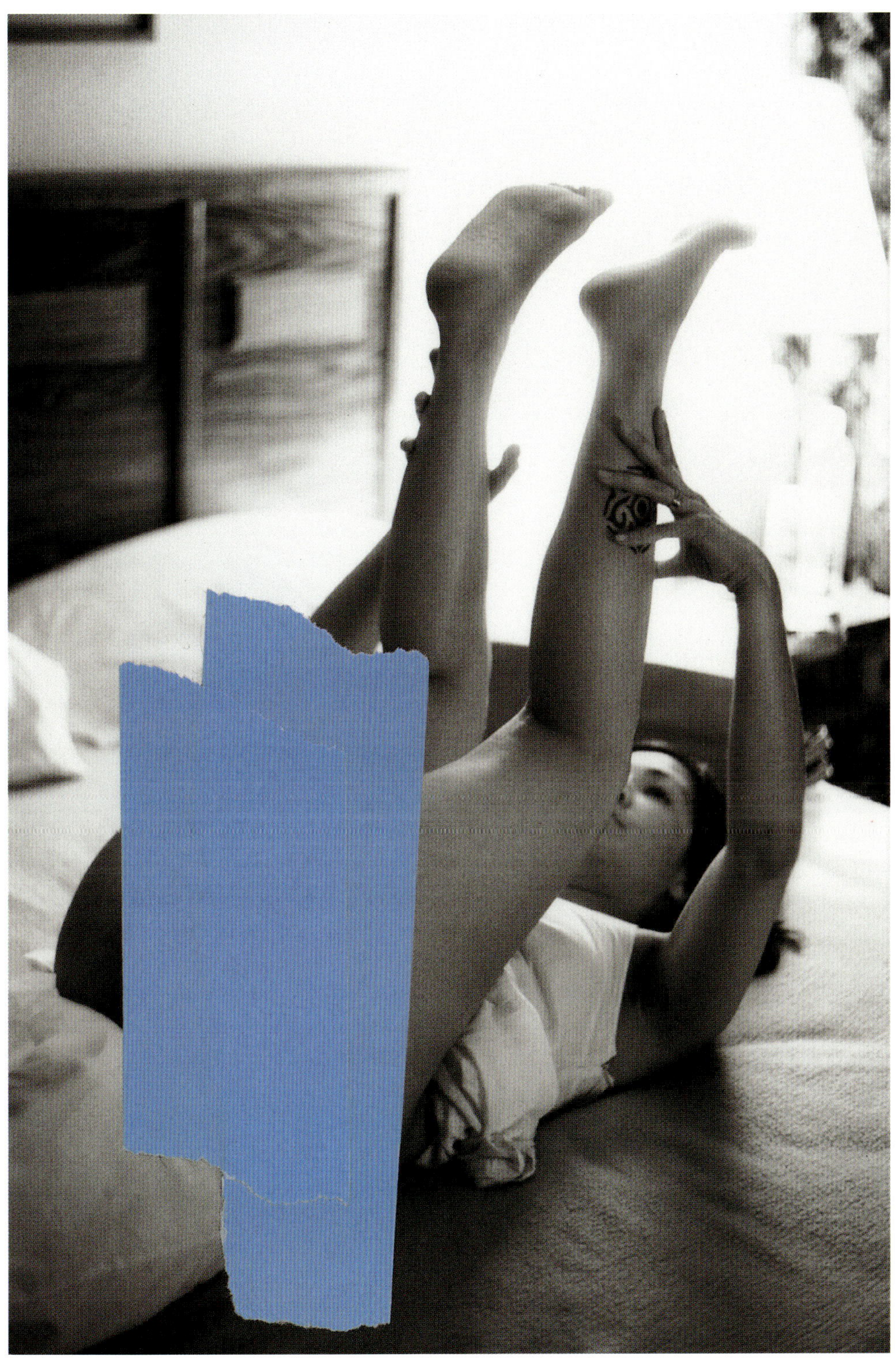

ET

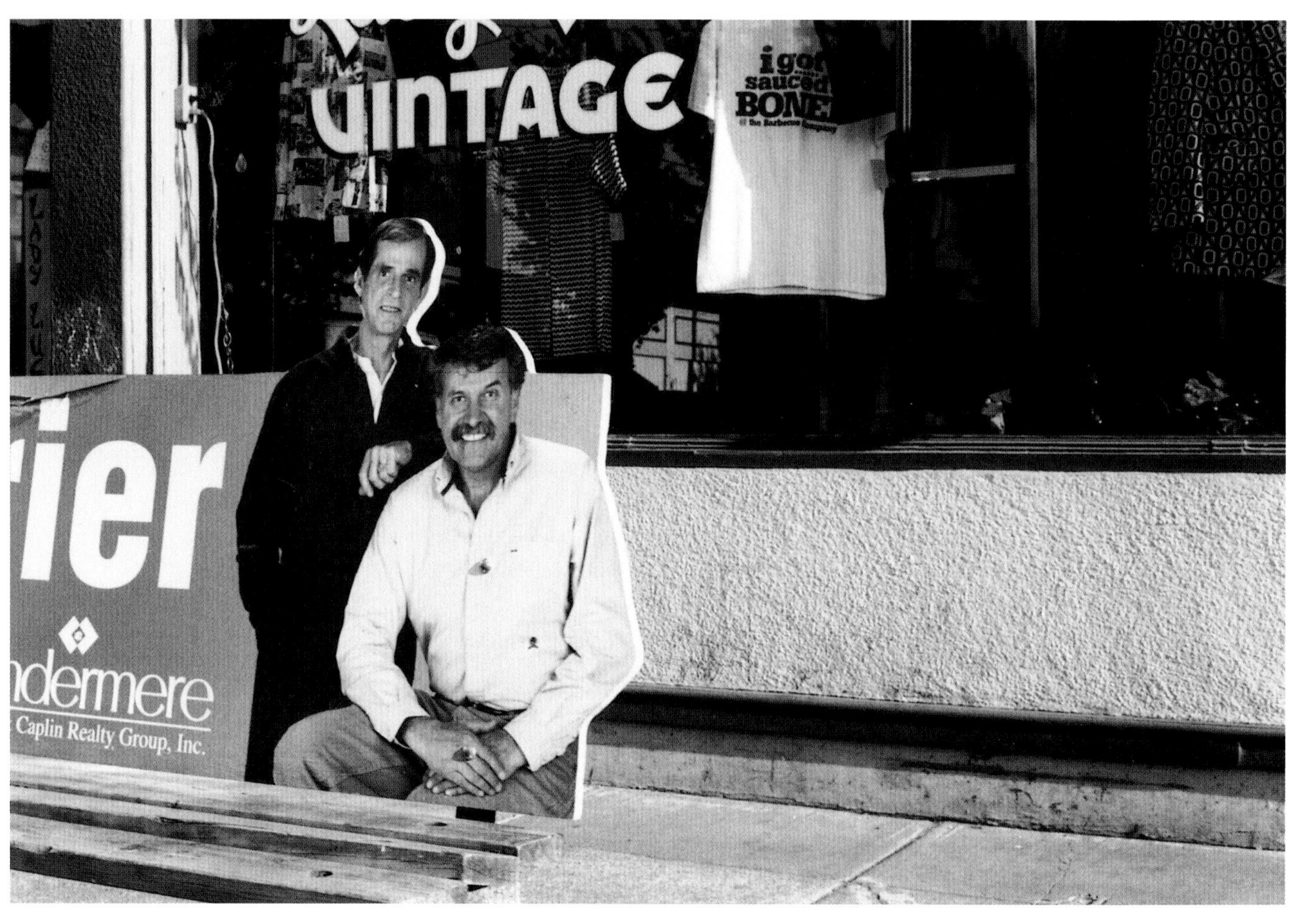

ET

TUALATIN

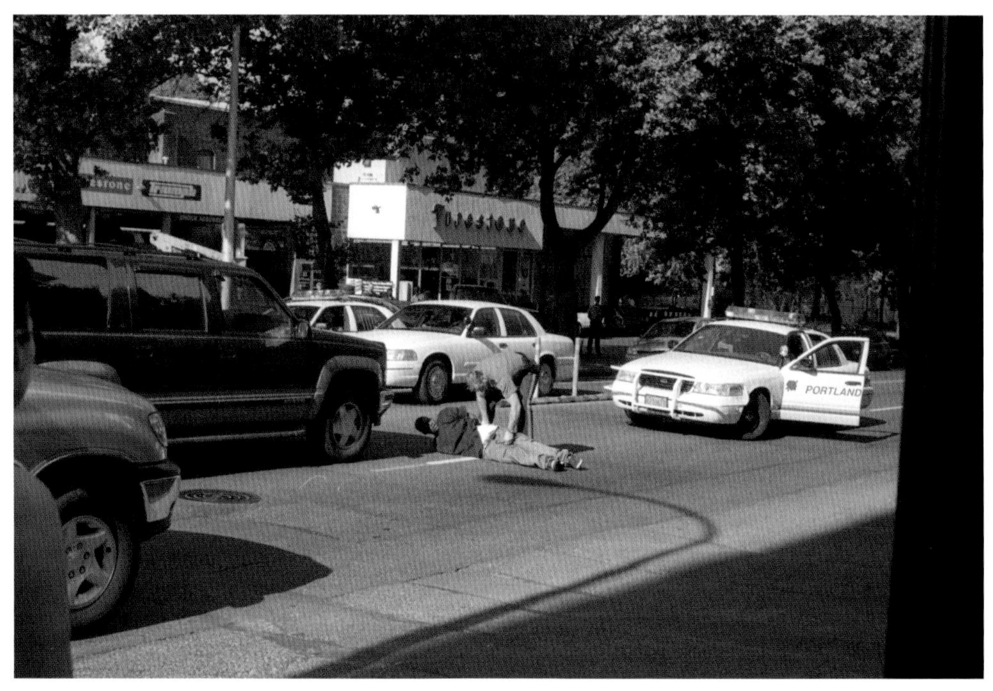

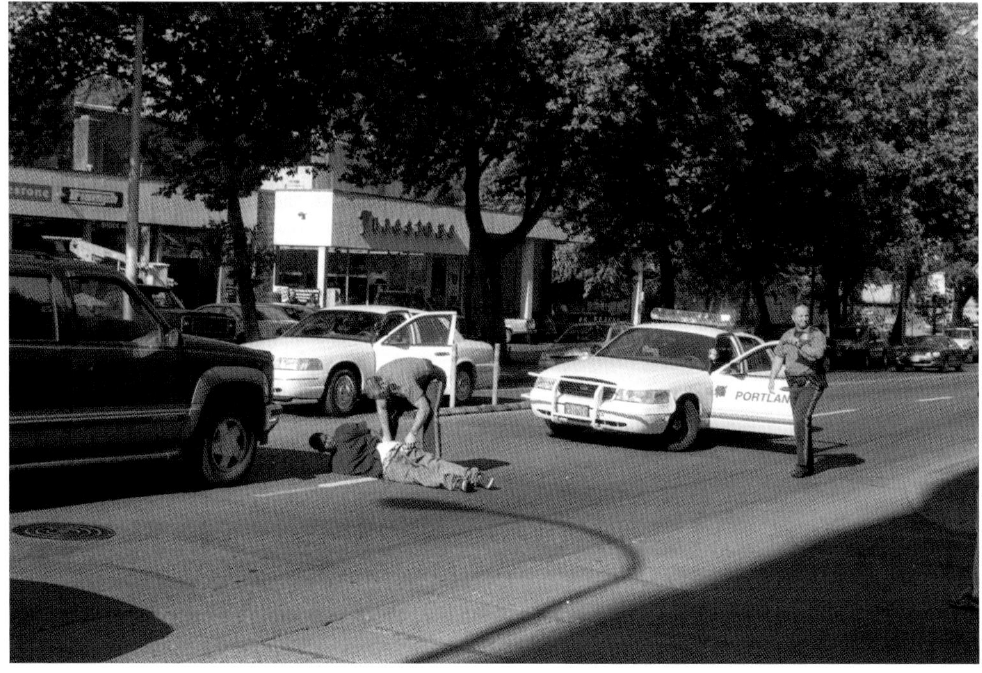

ET

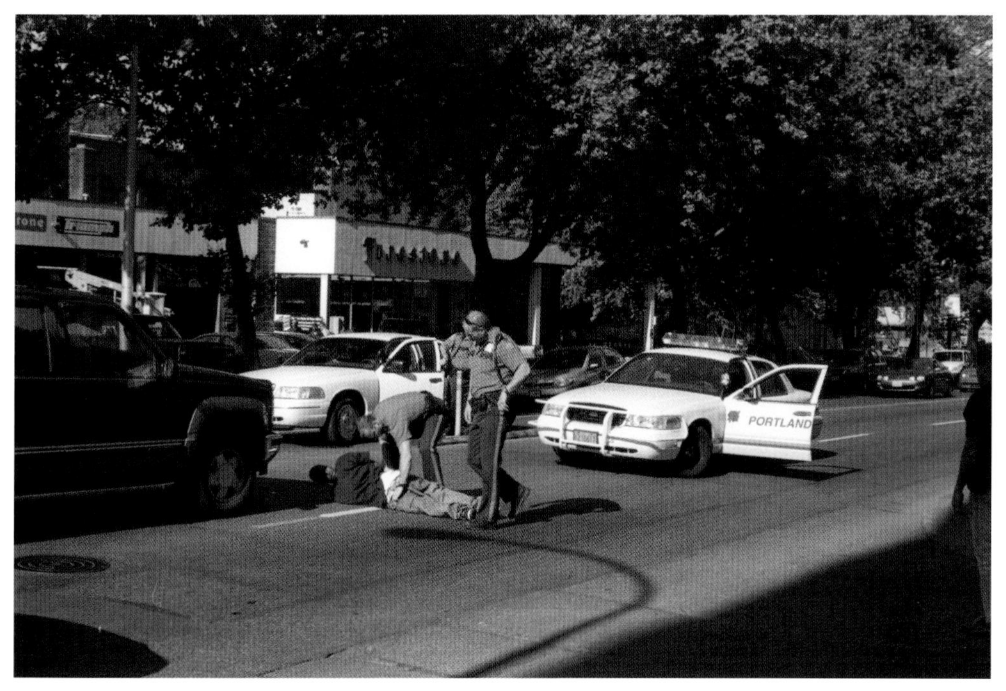

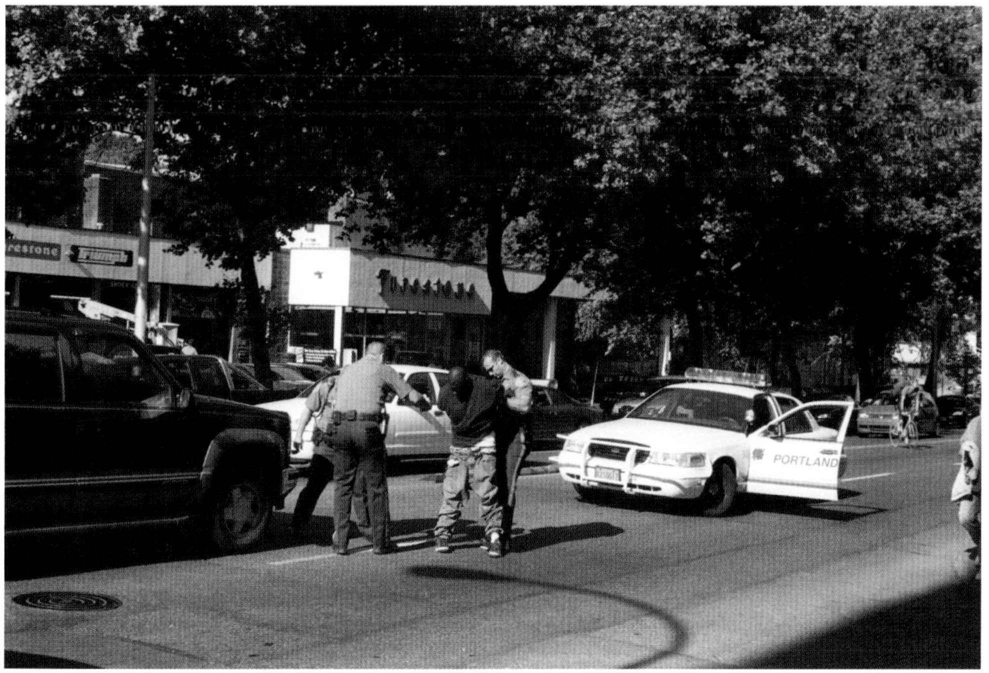

ET

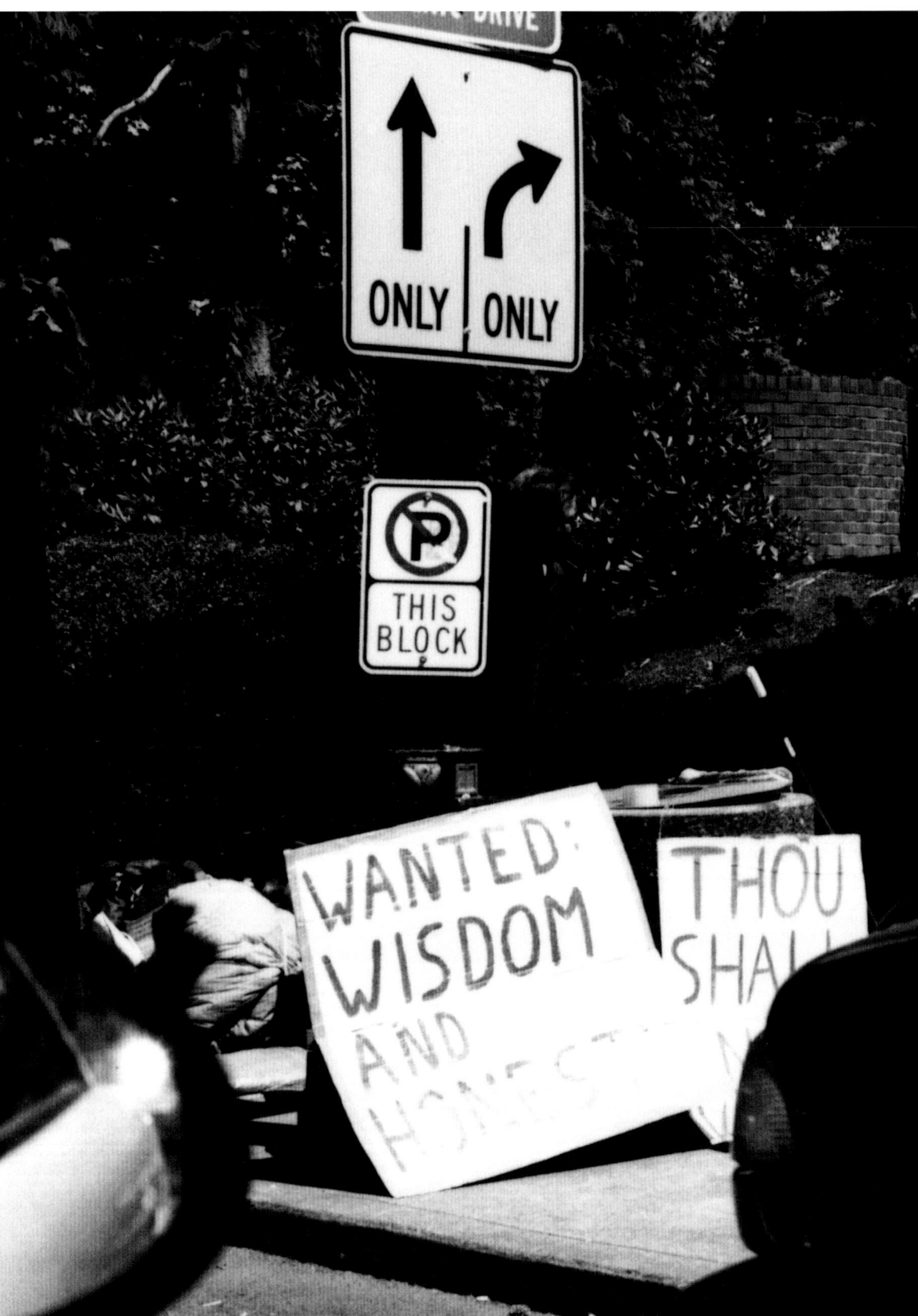
DRIVE
ONLY
ONLY
THIS
BLOCK
WANTED:
WISDOM
AND
THOU

ET

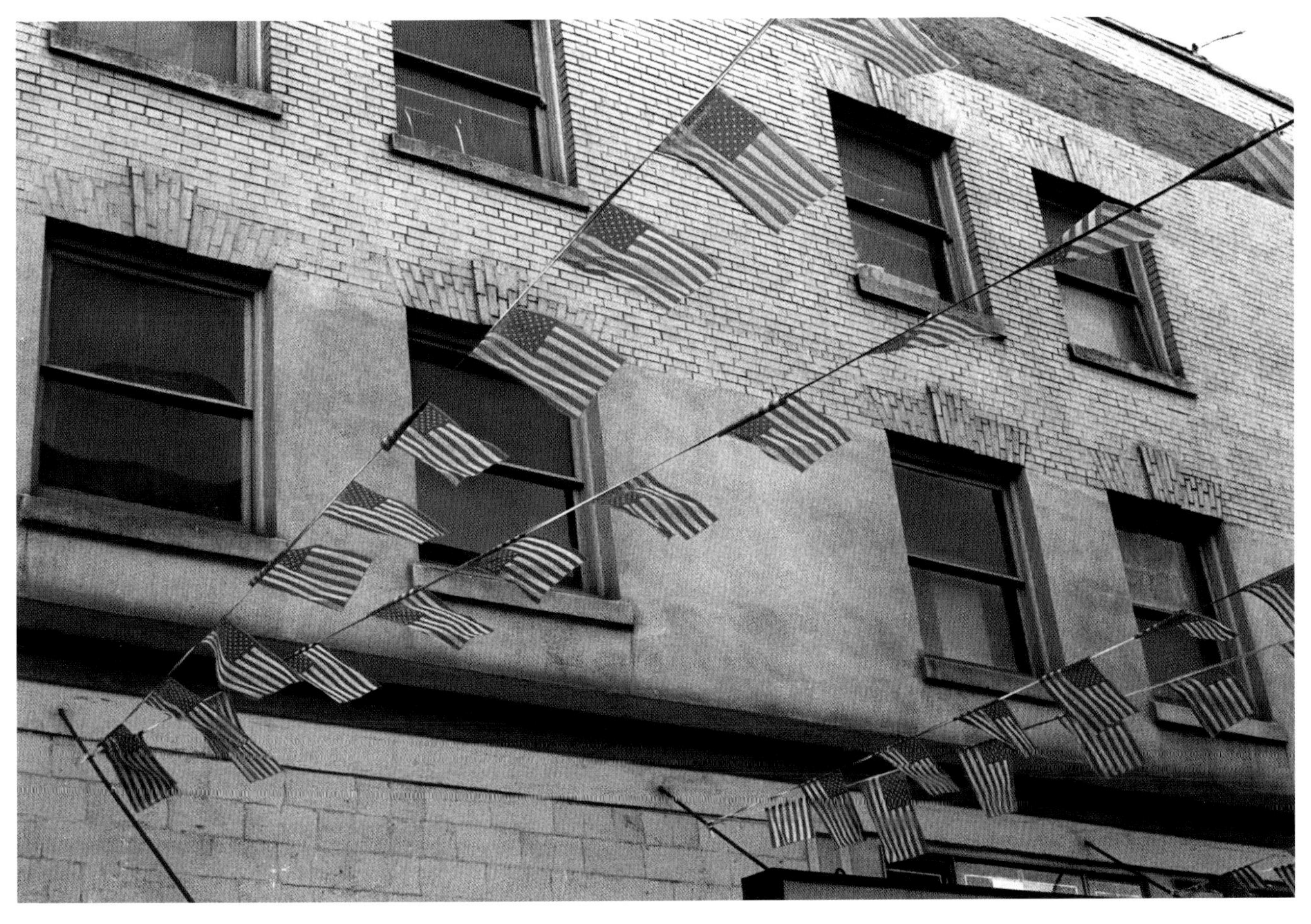

ET

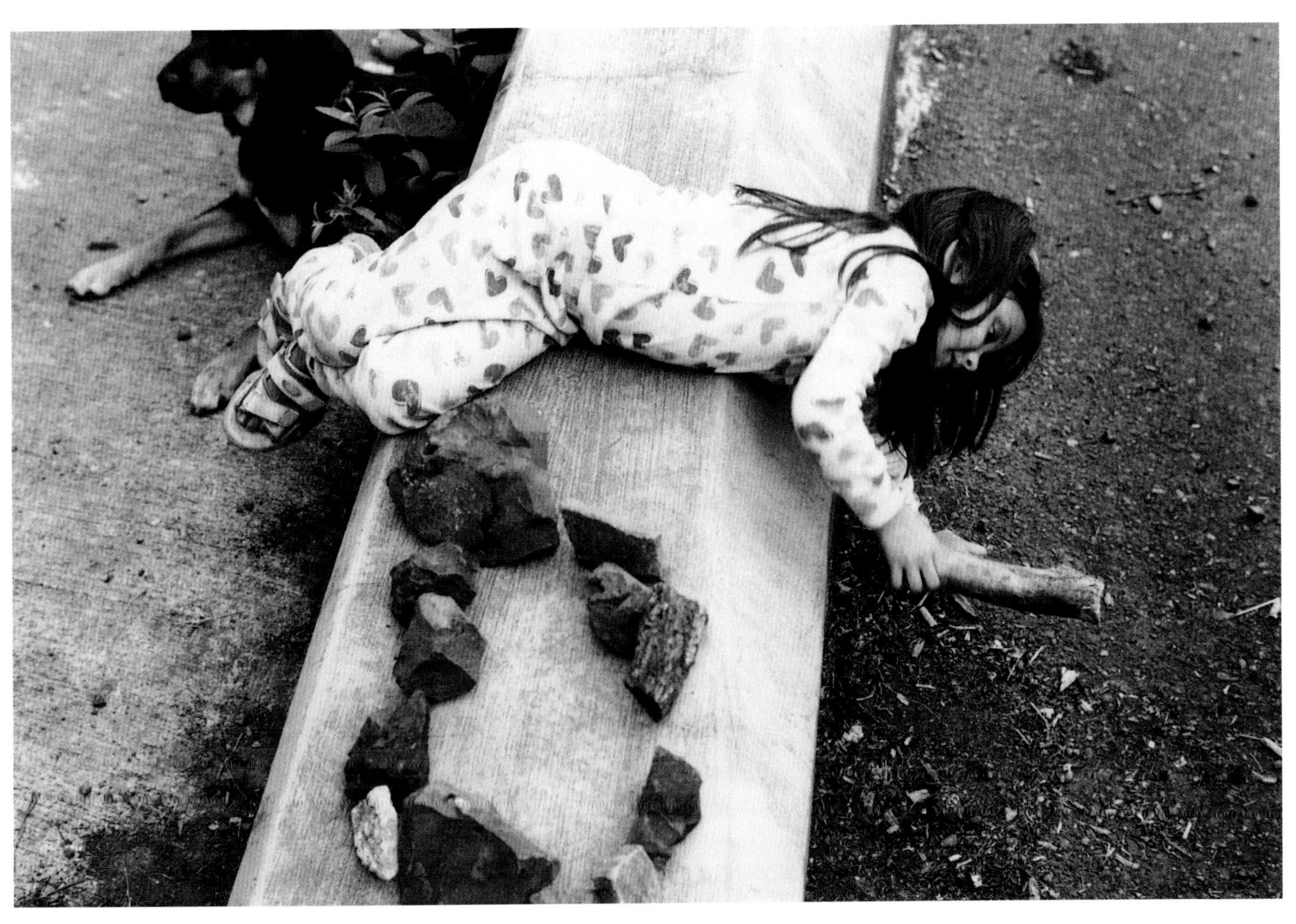

ET

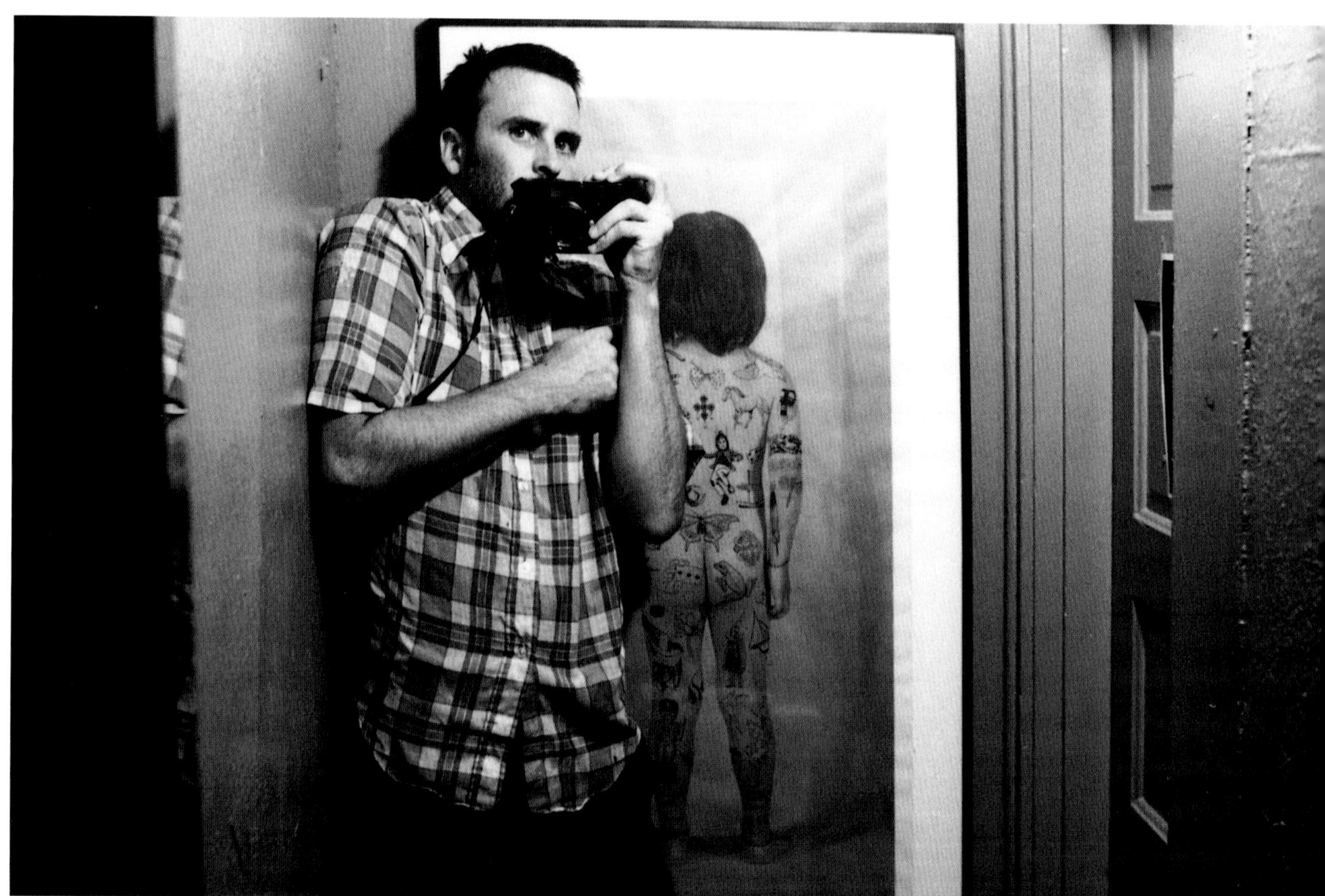

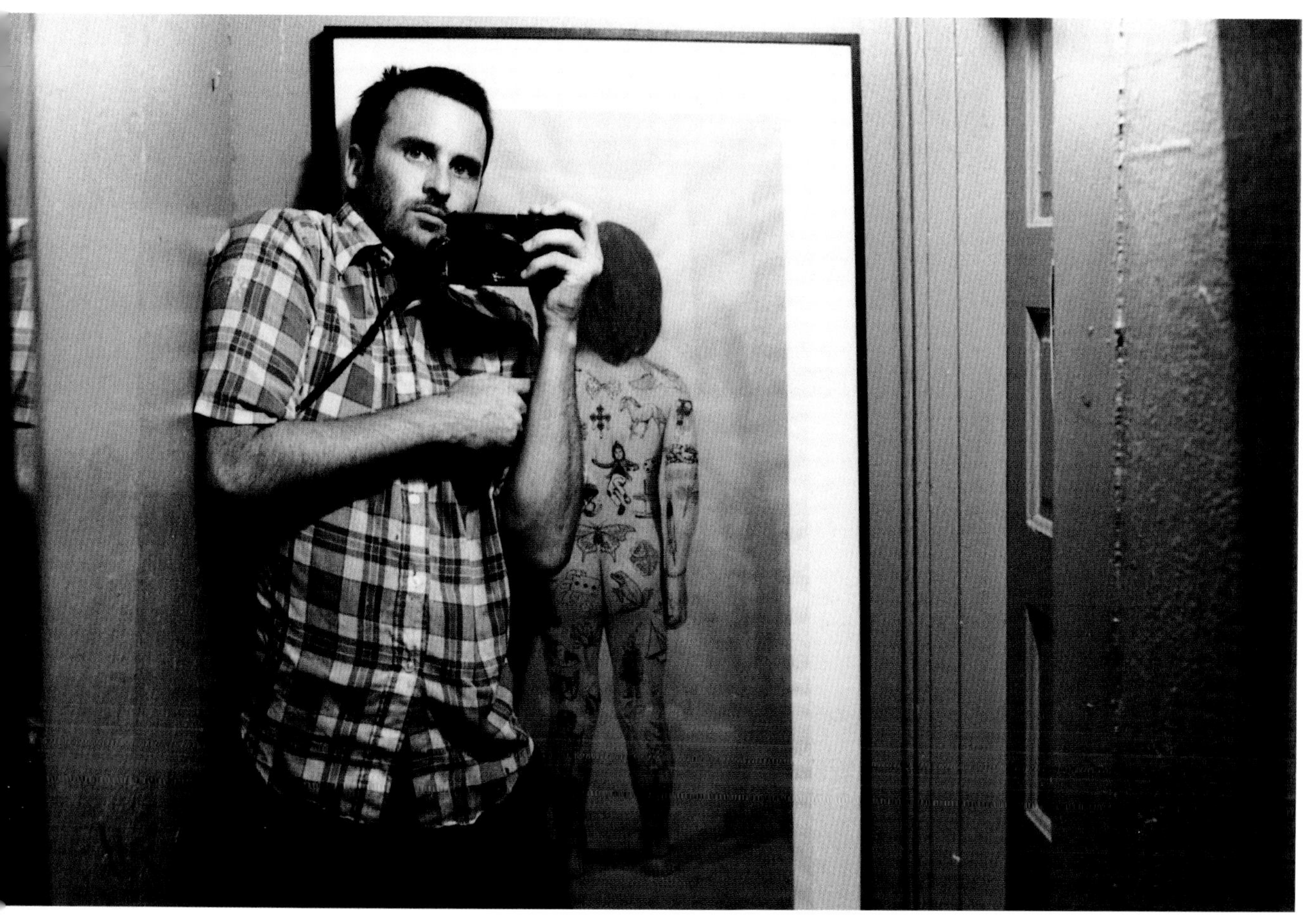

ET

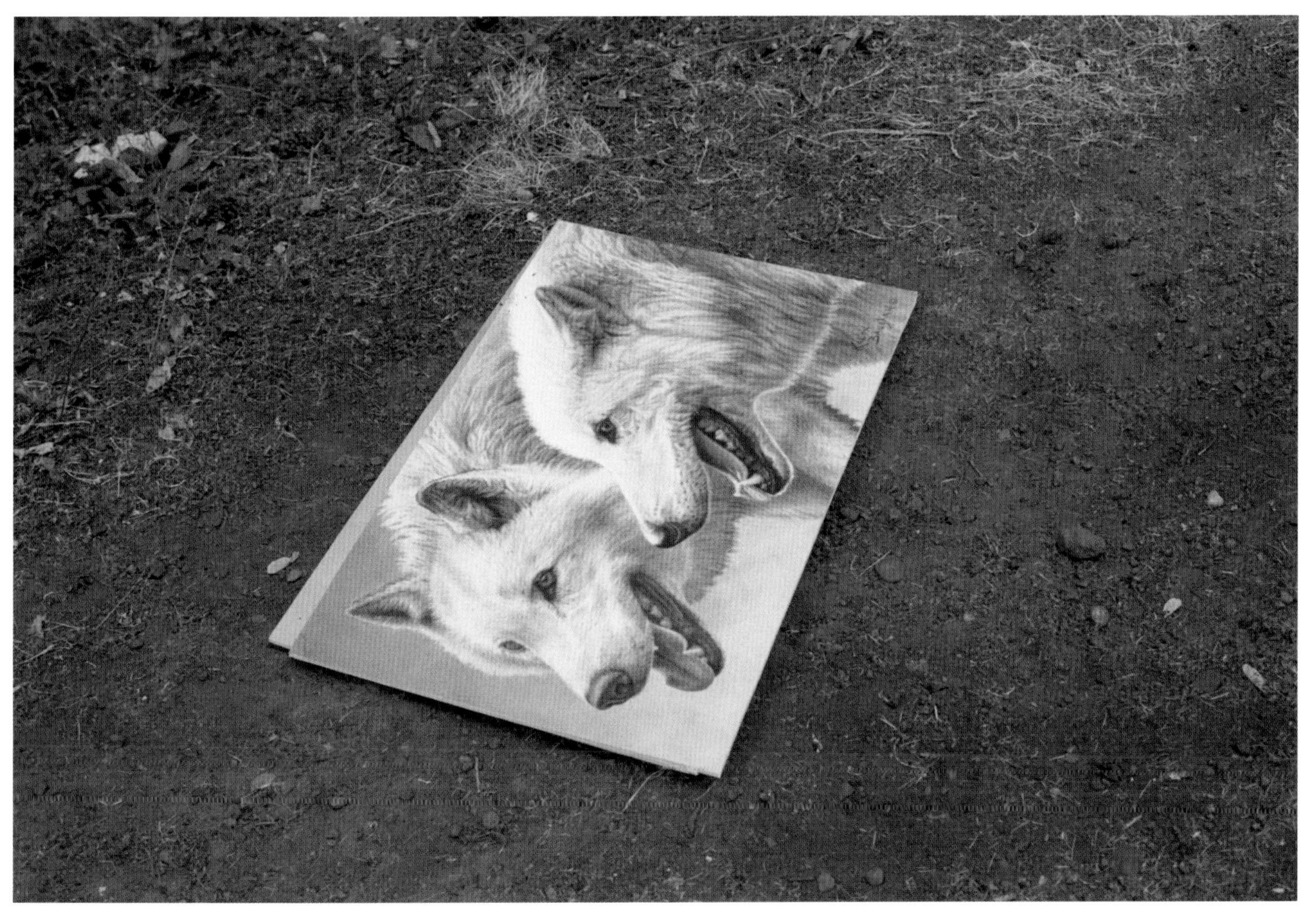

TC

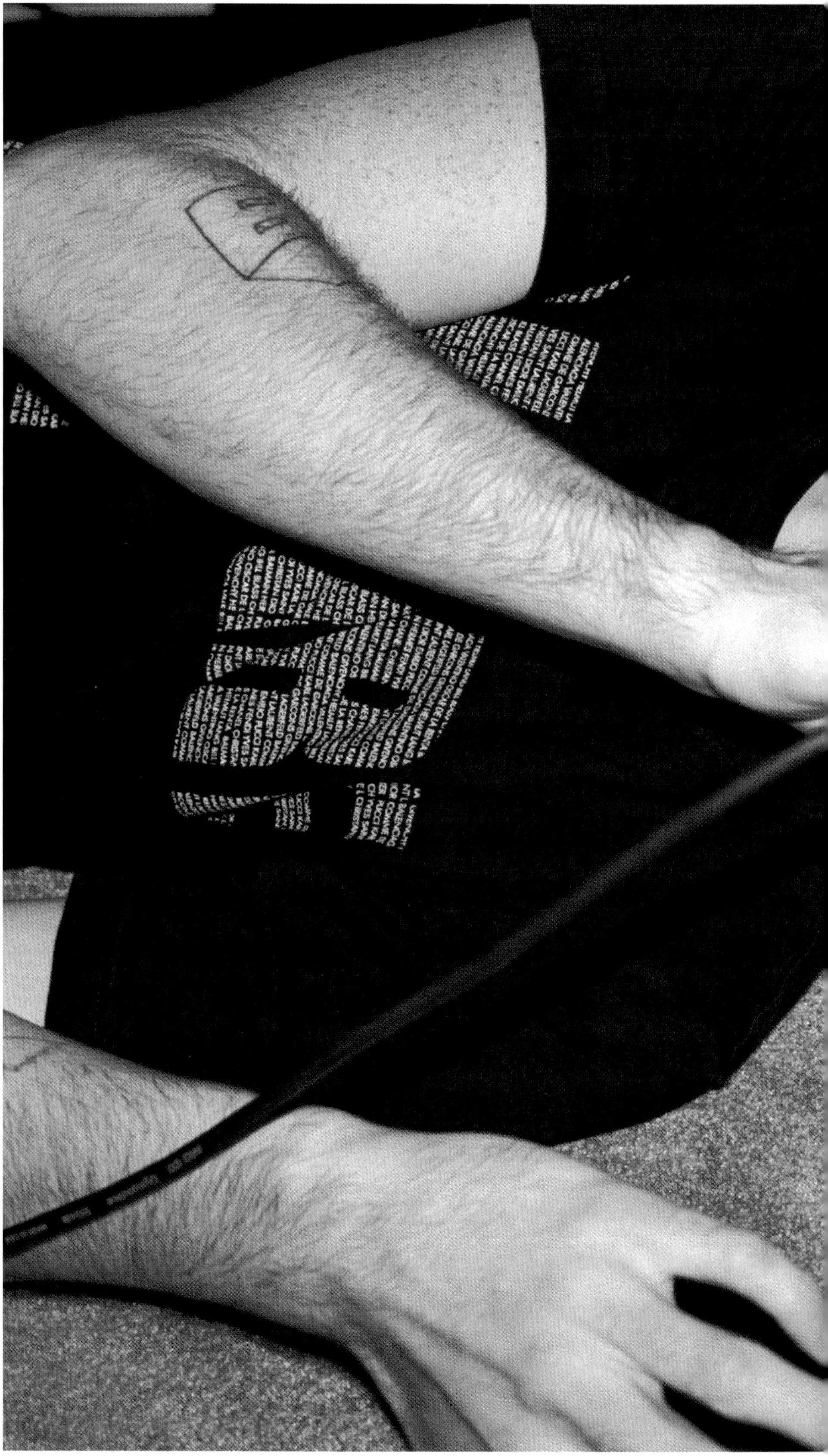

TC

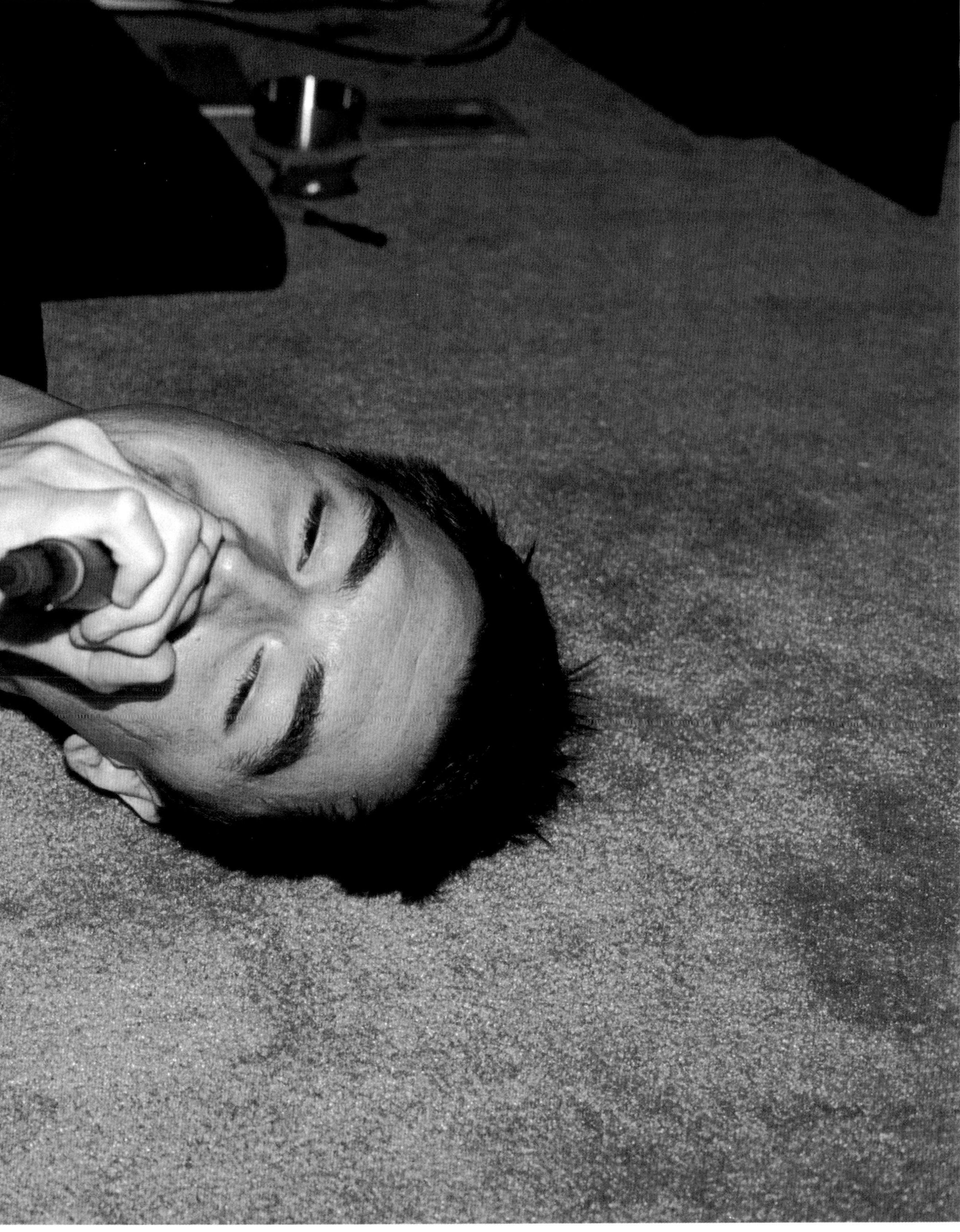

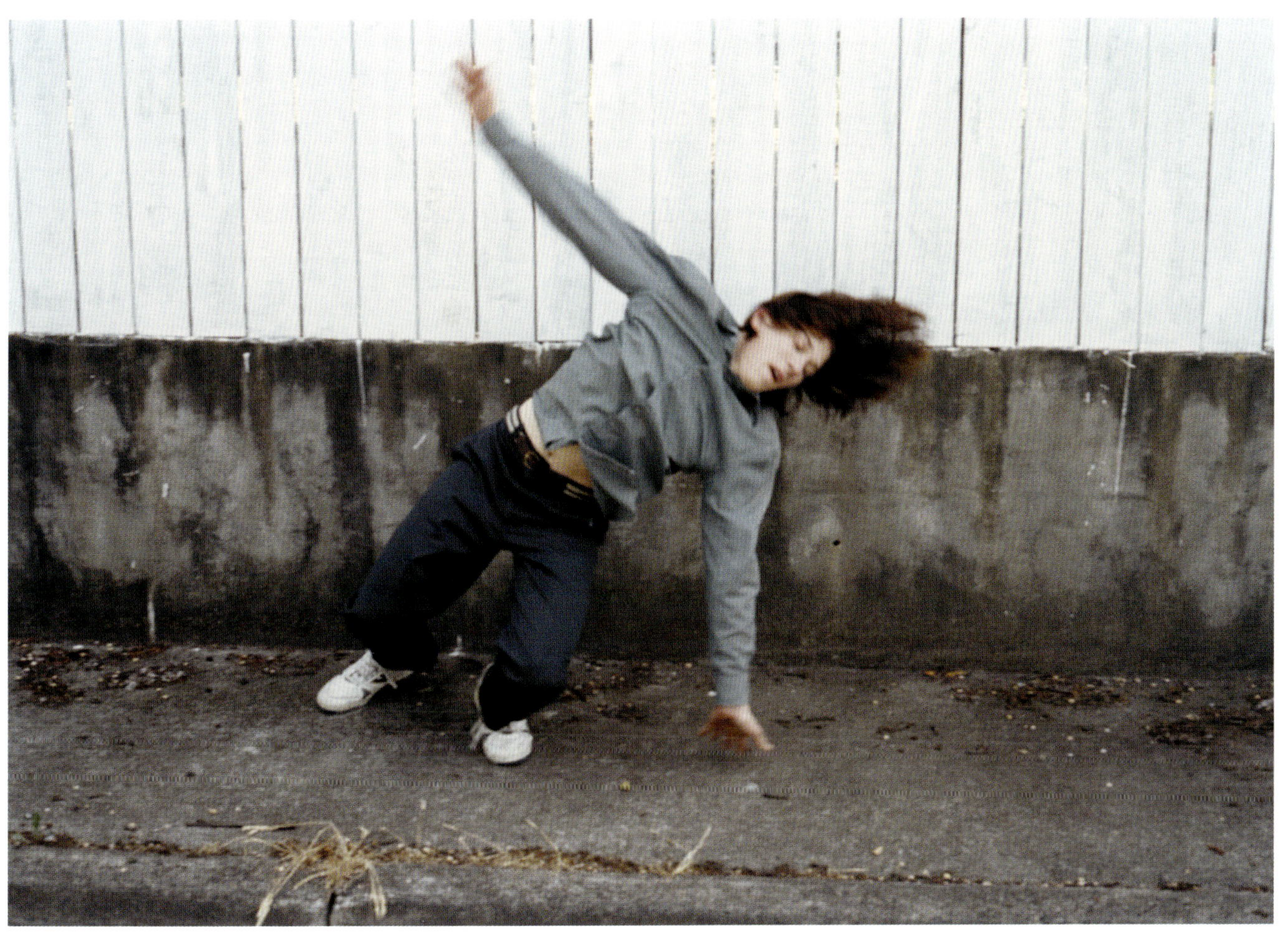

TC

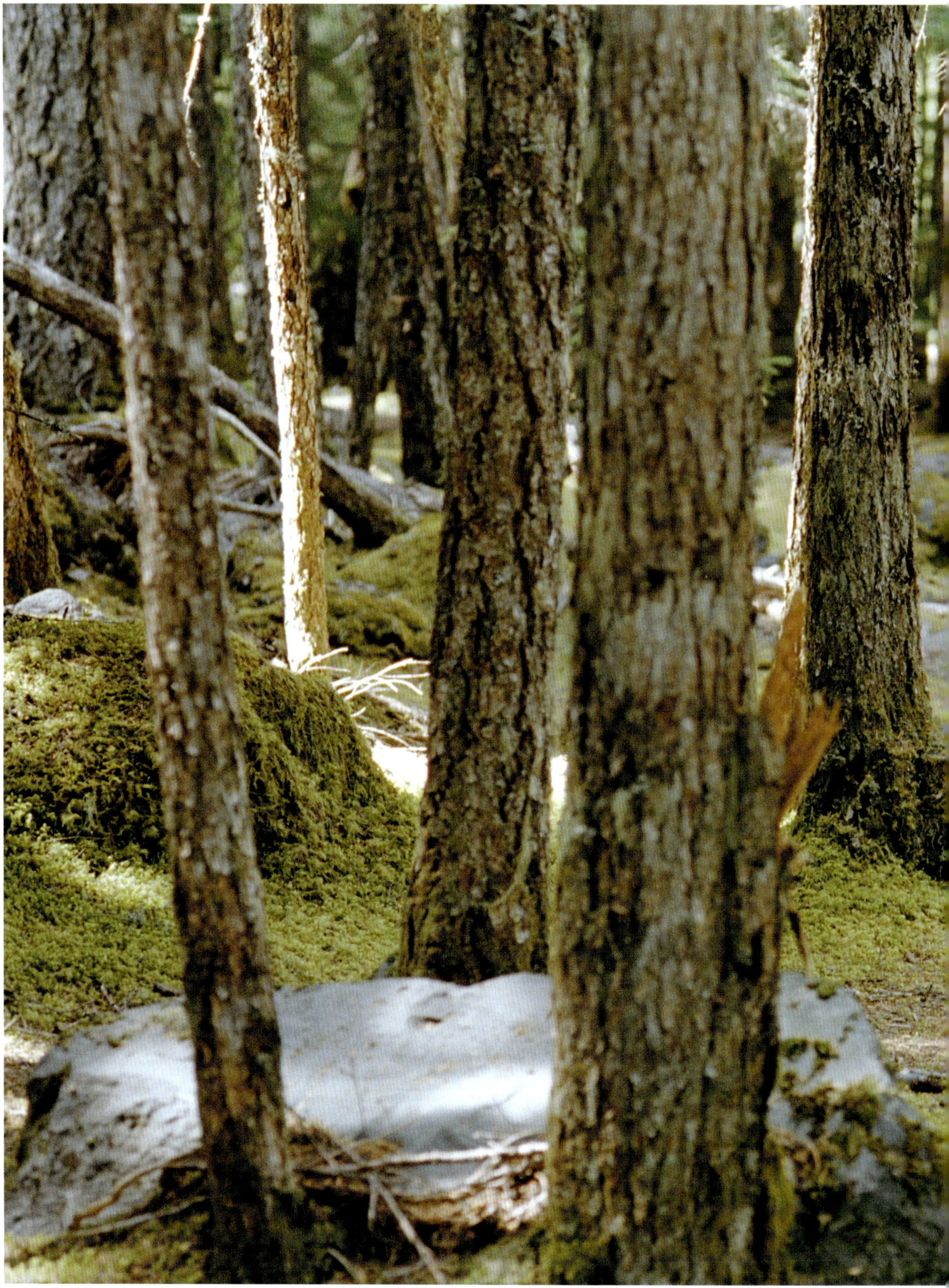

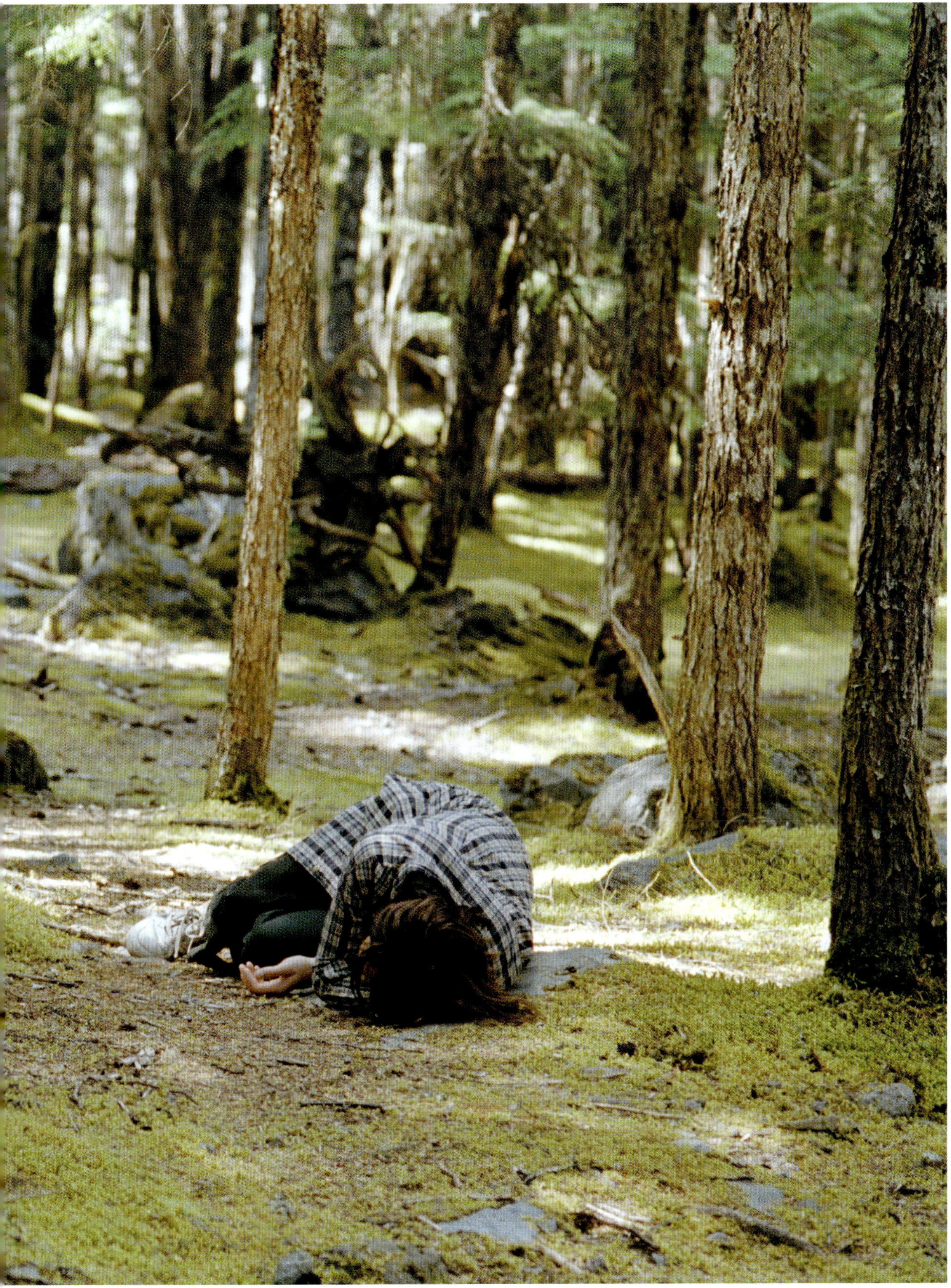

TC

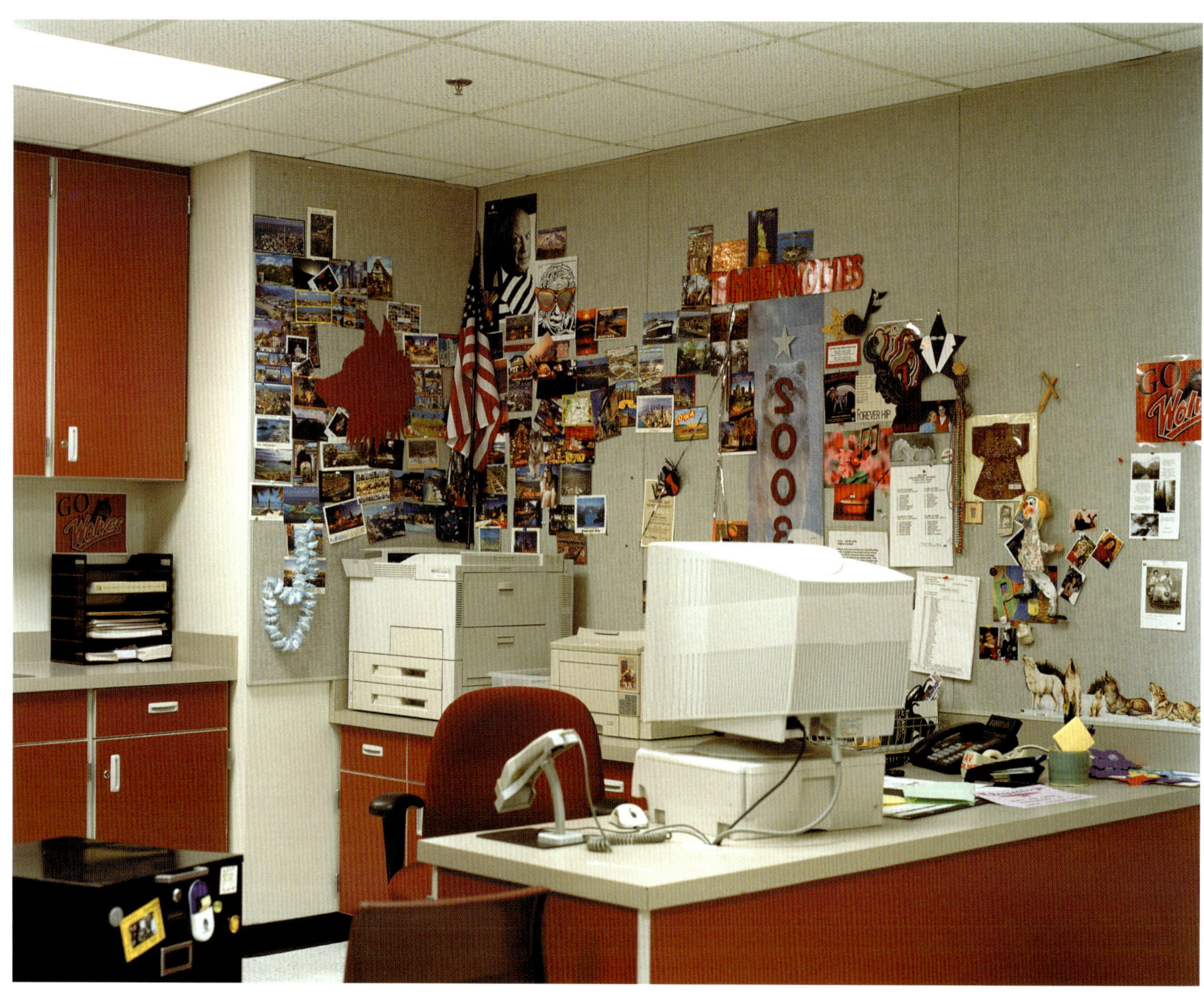

TC

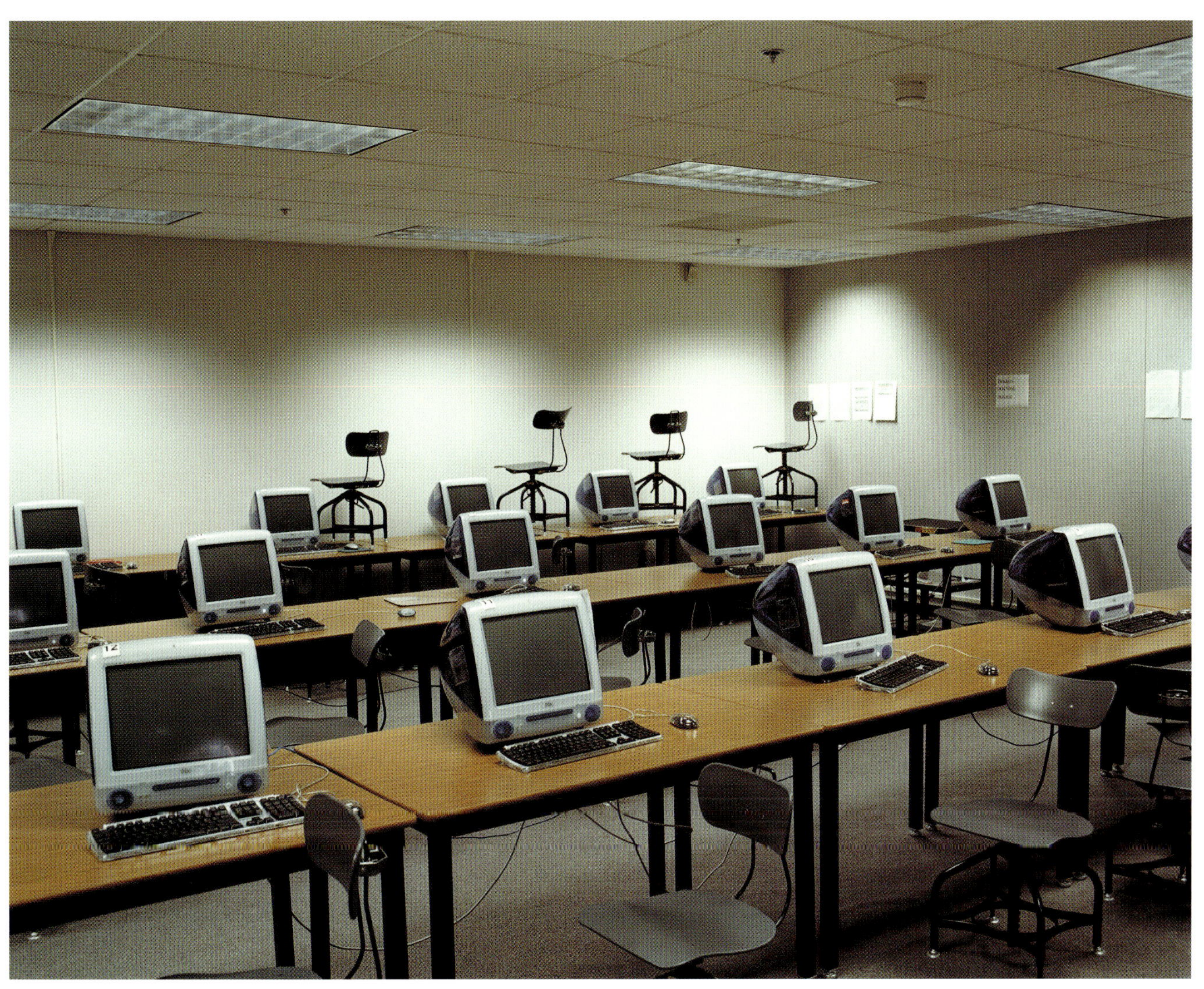

TC

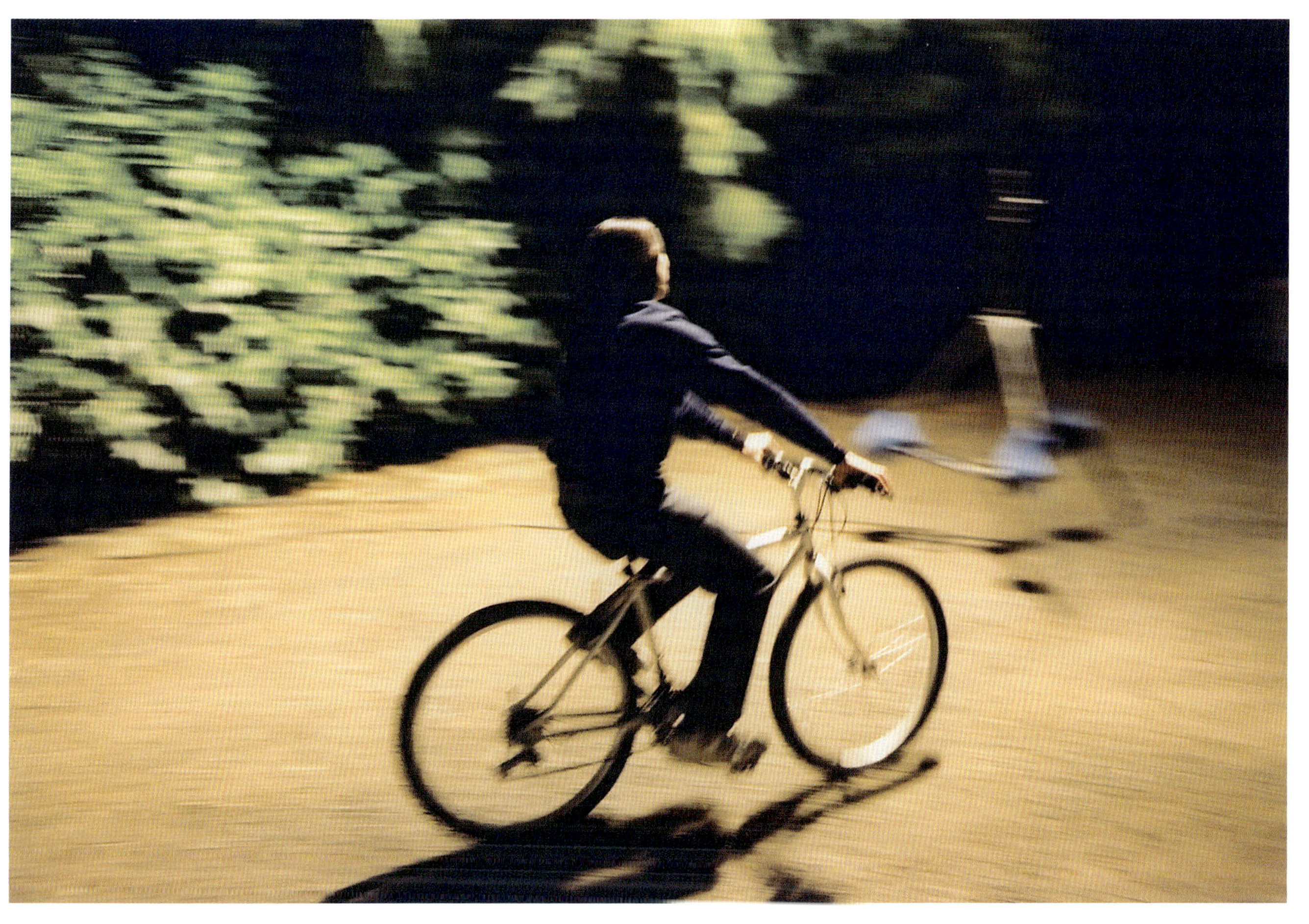

RM

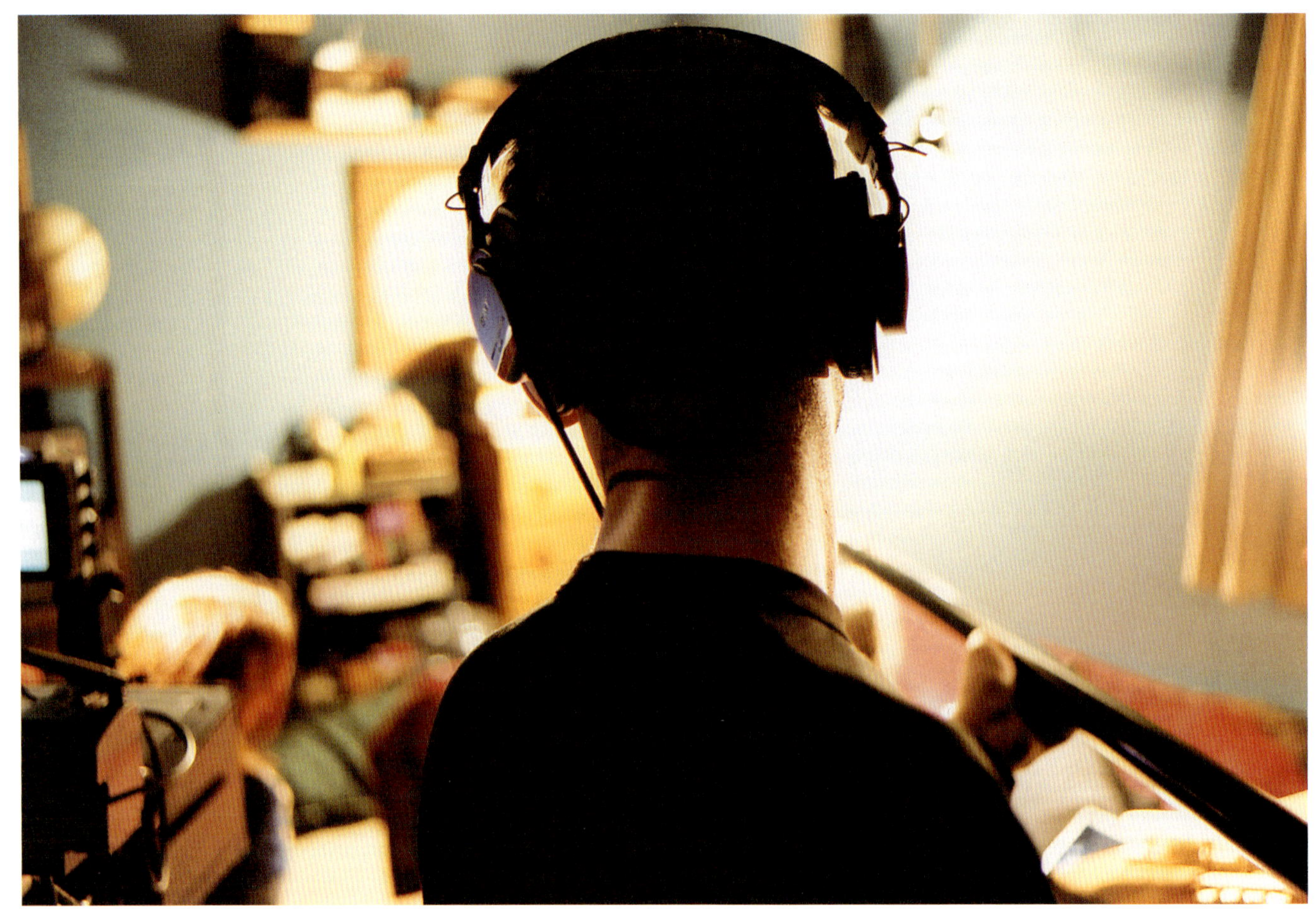

RM

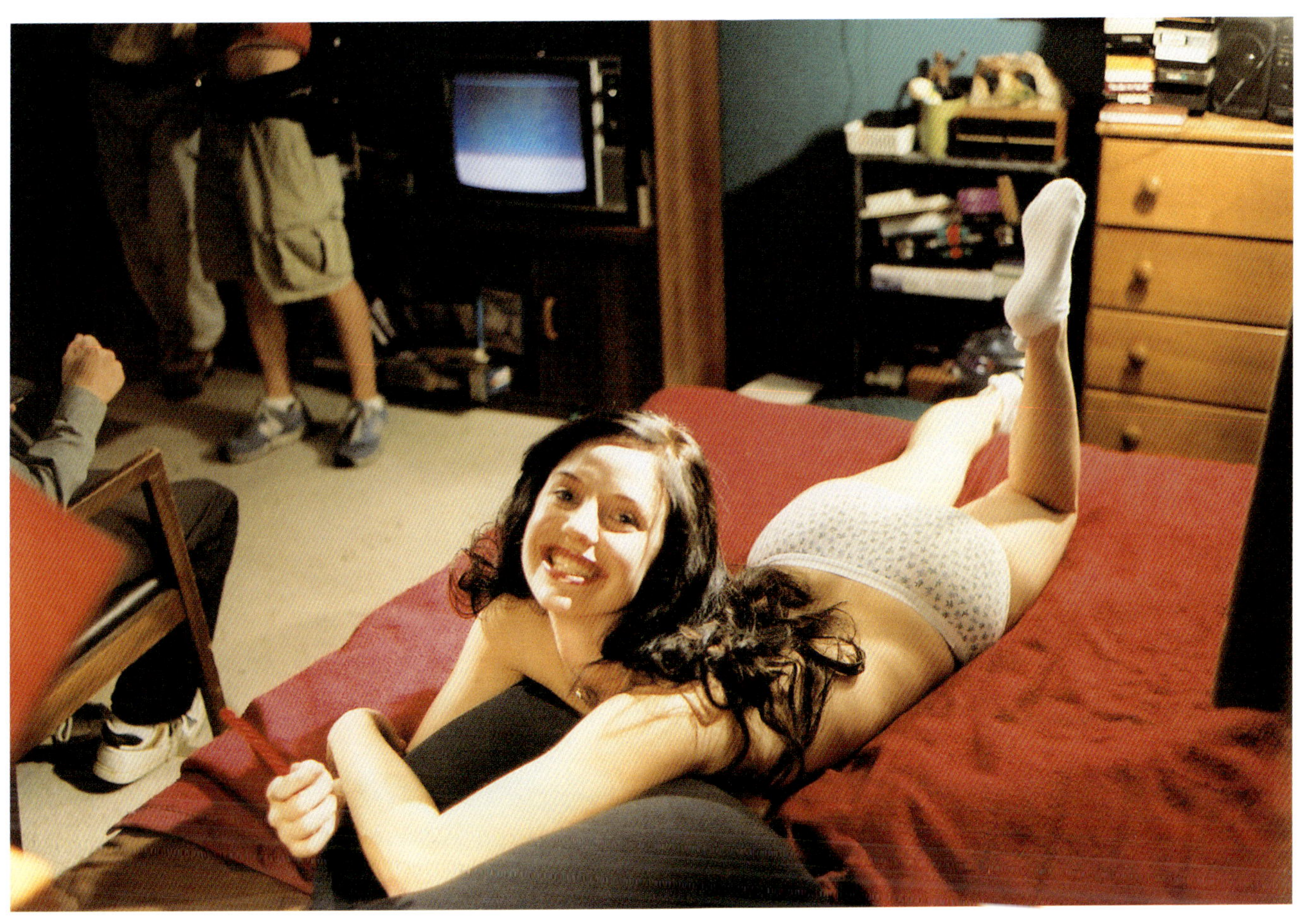

RM

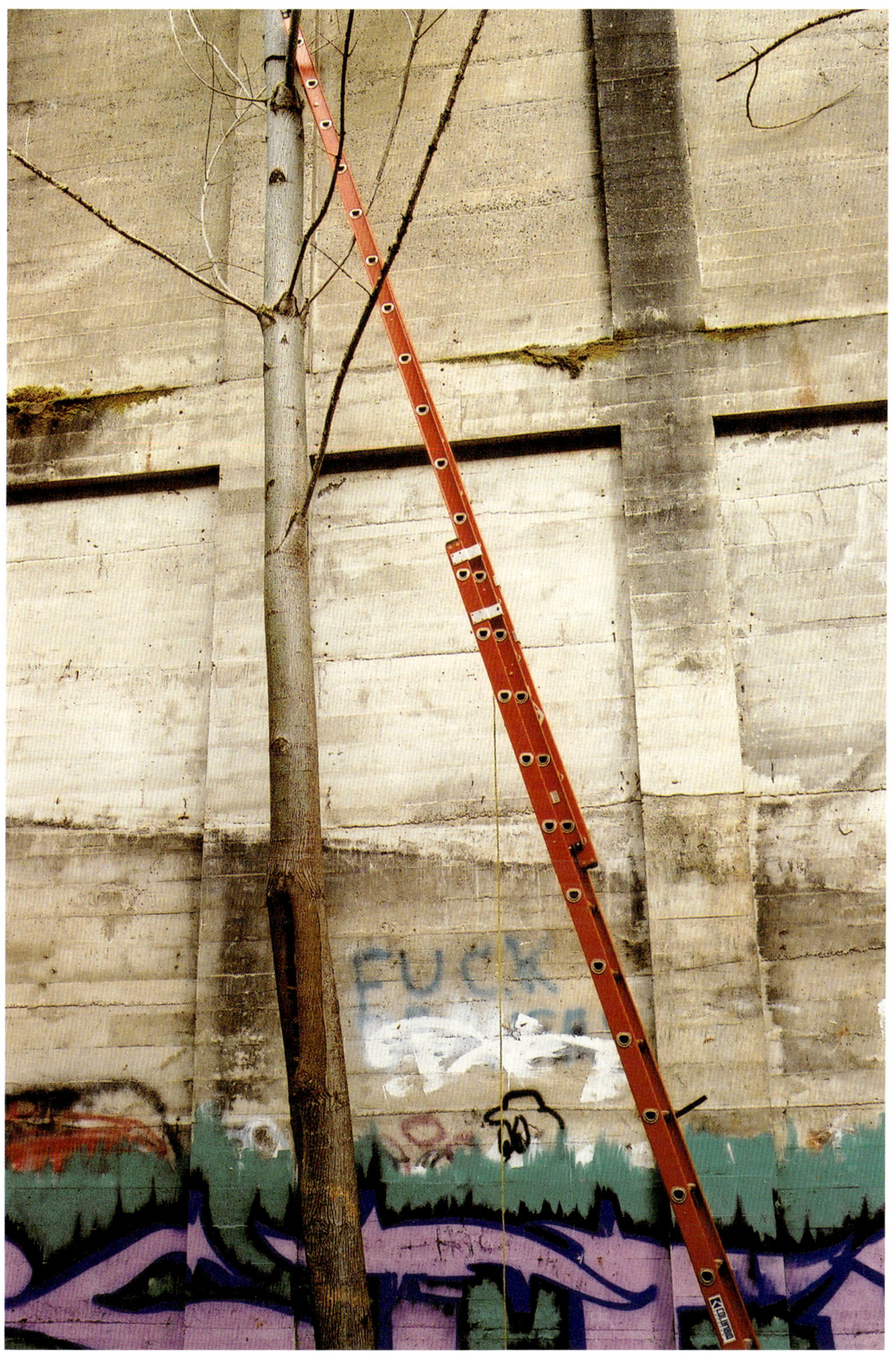

RM

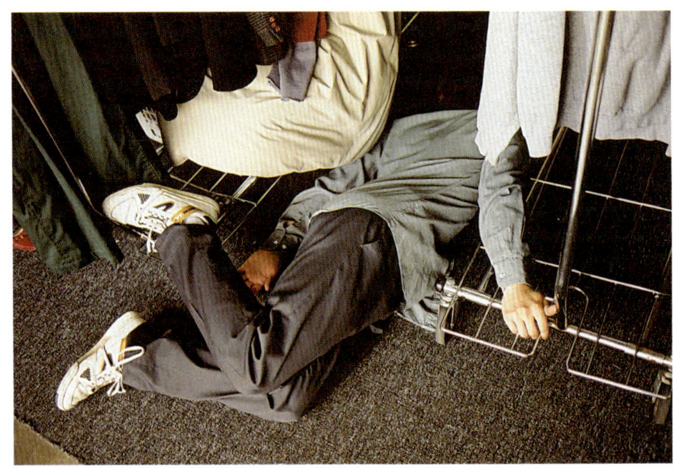

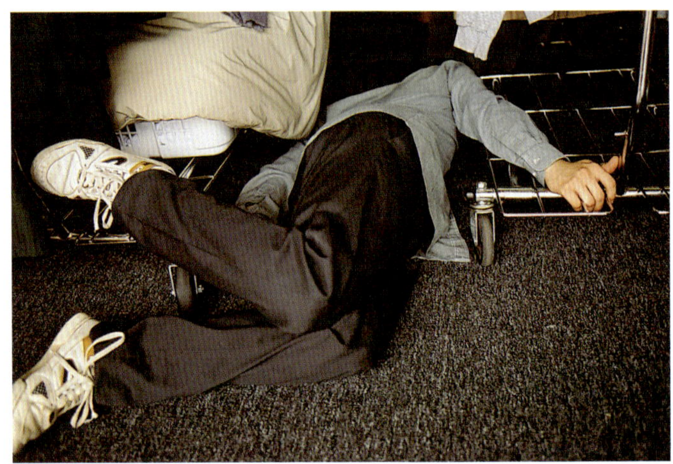

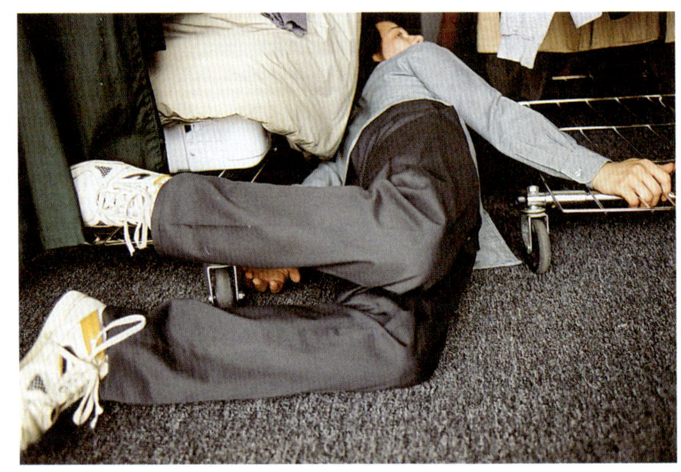

RM

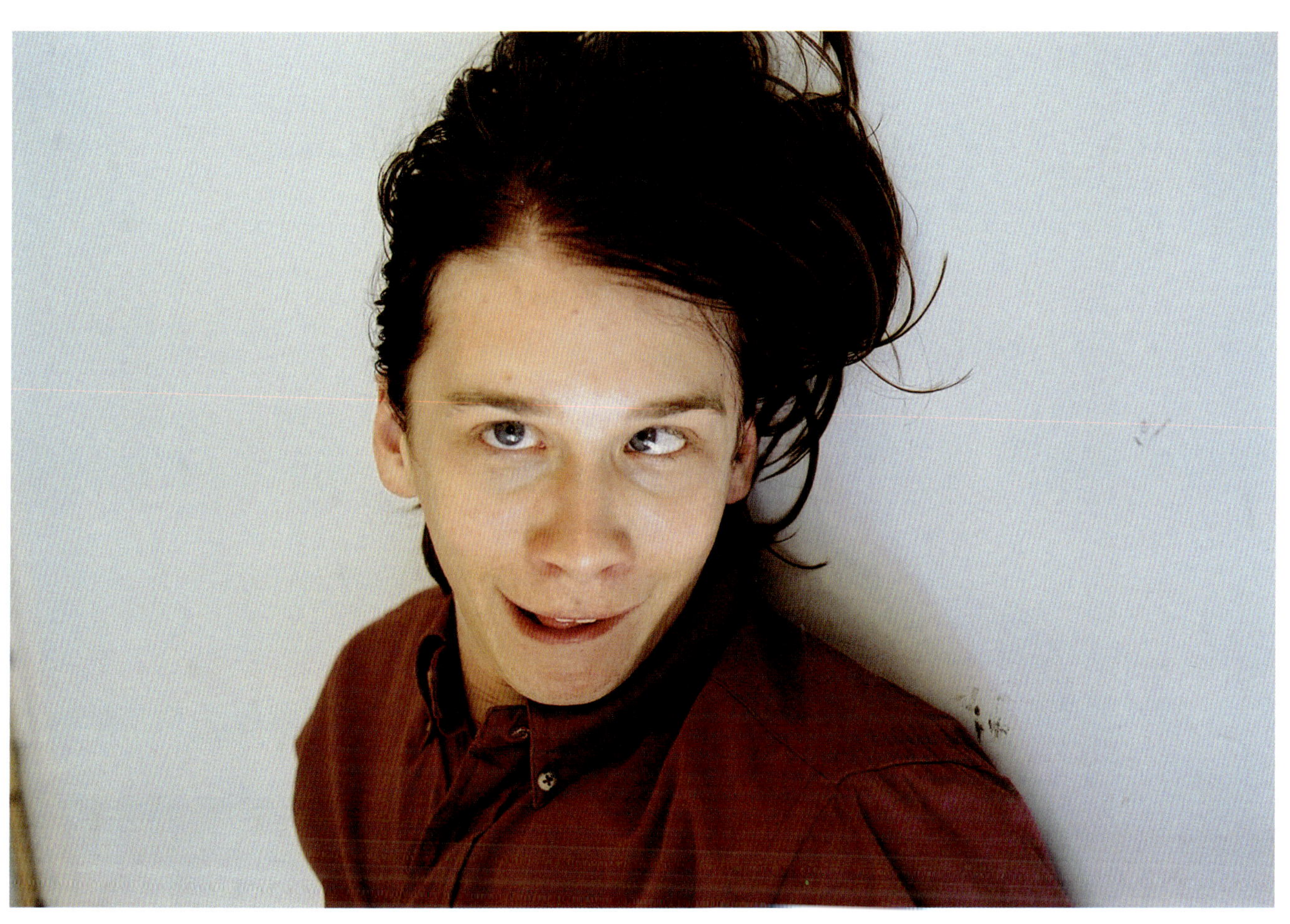

RM

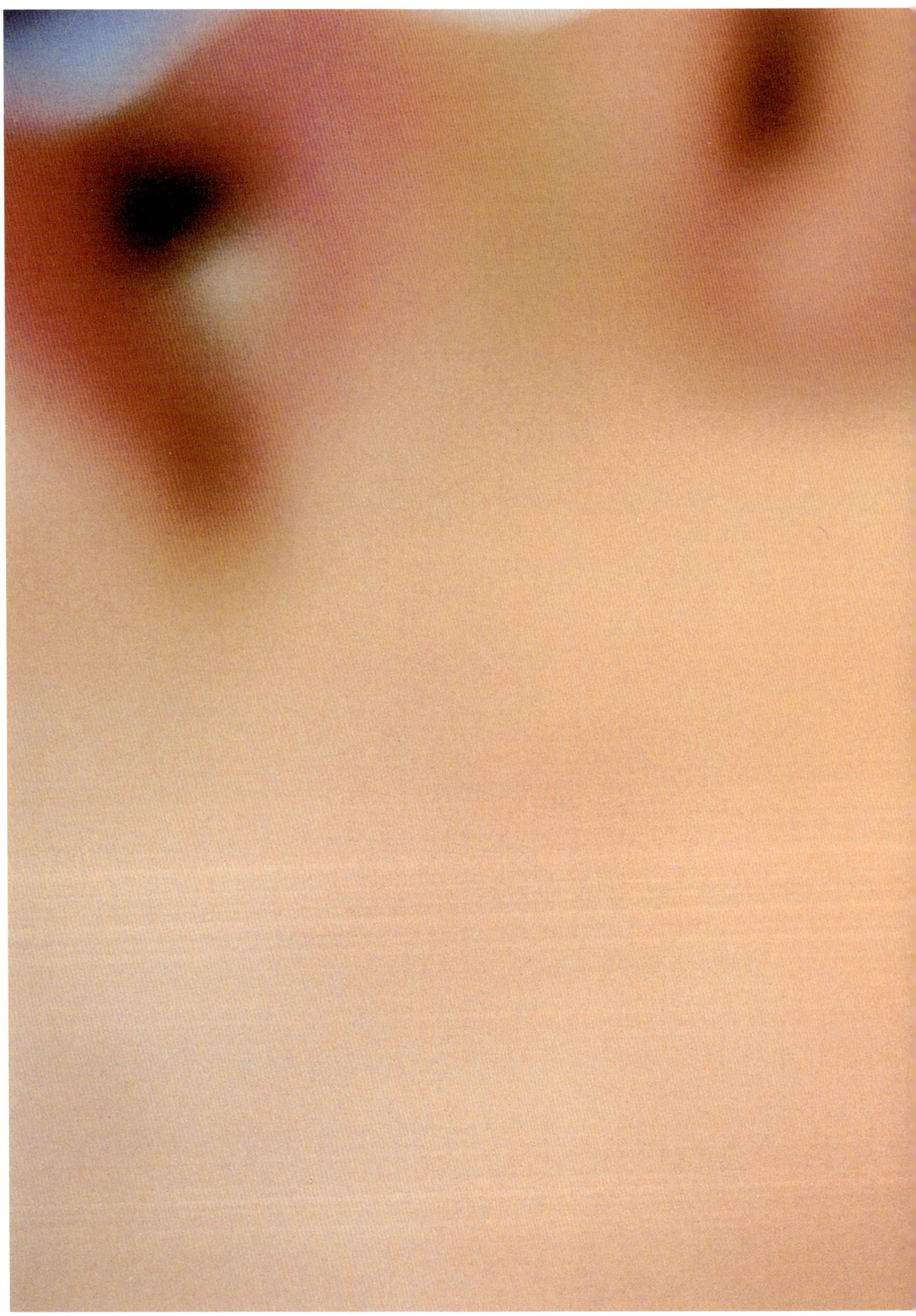

RM

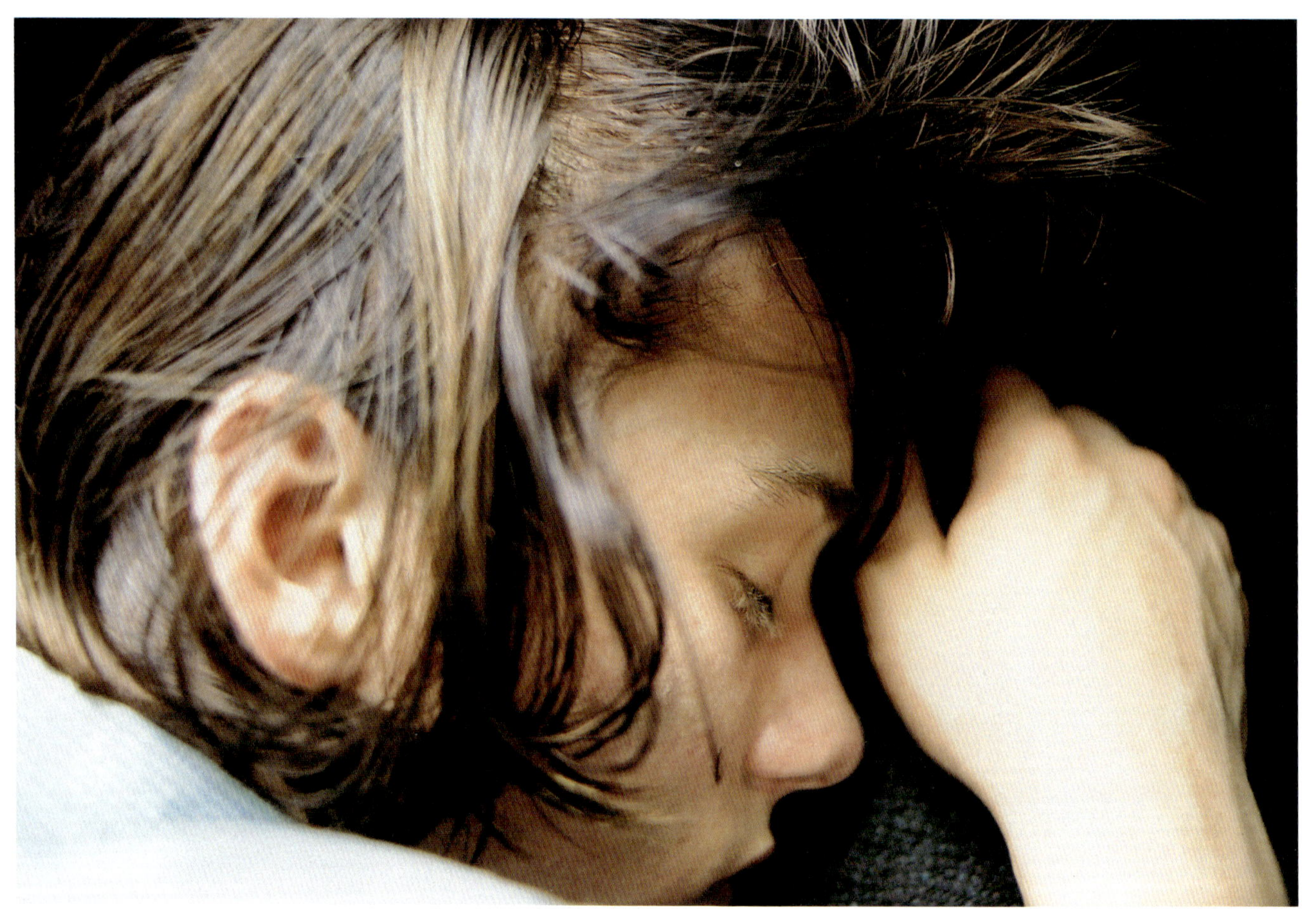

RM

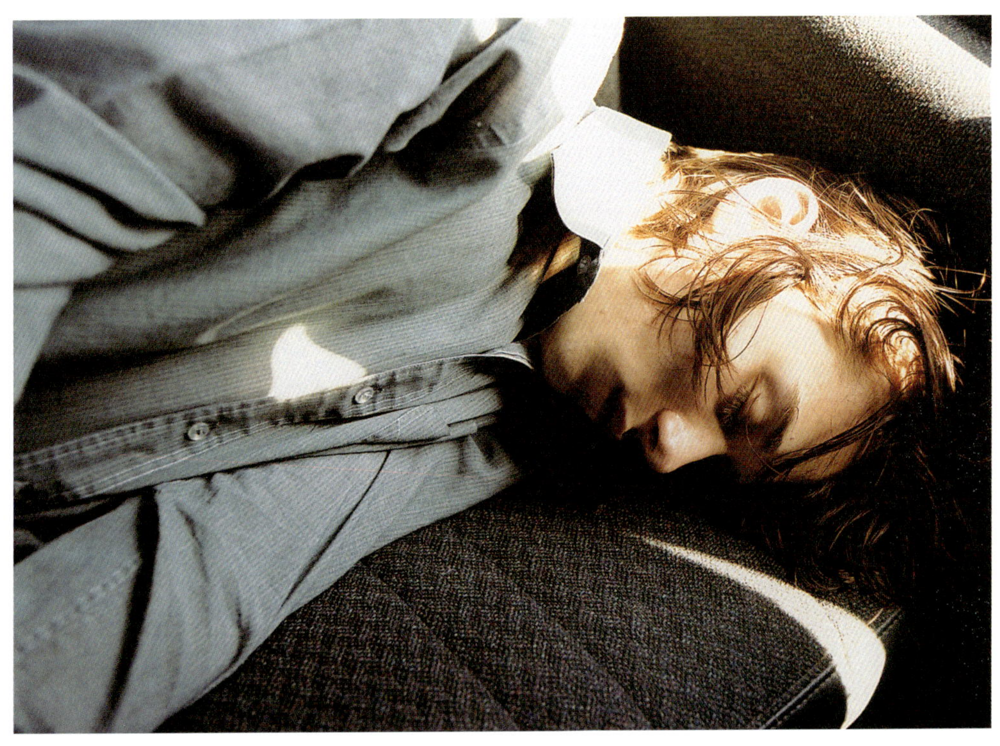

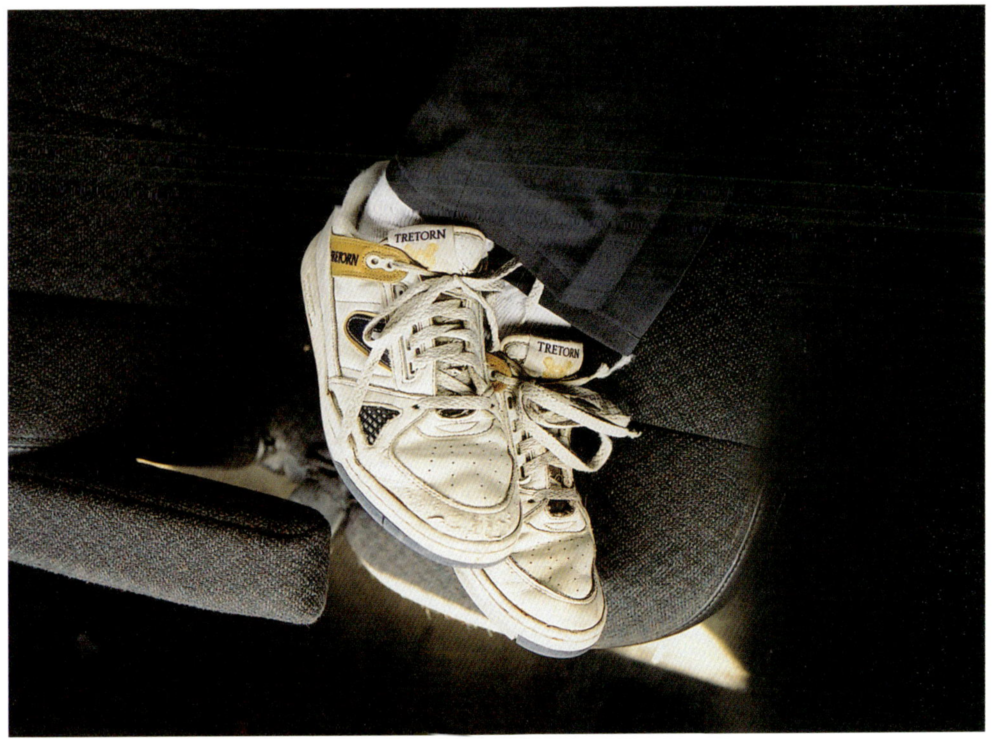

RM

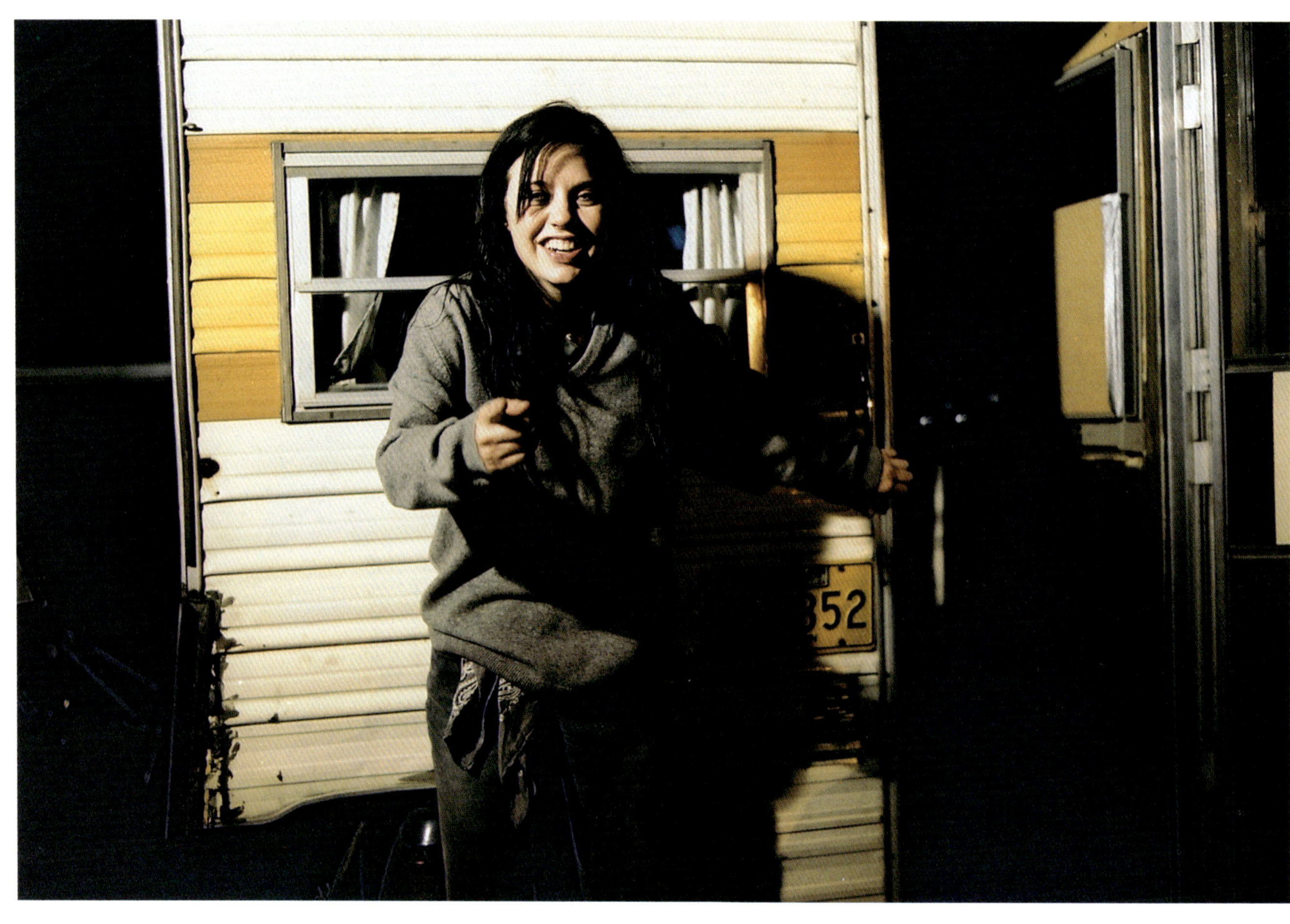

RM

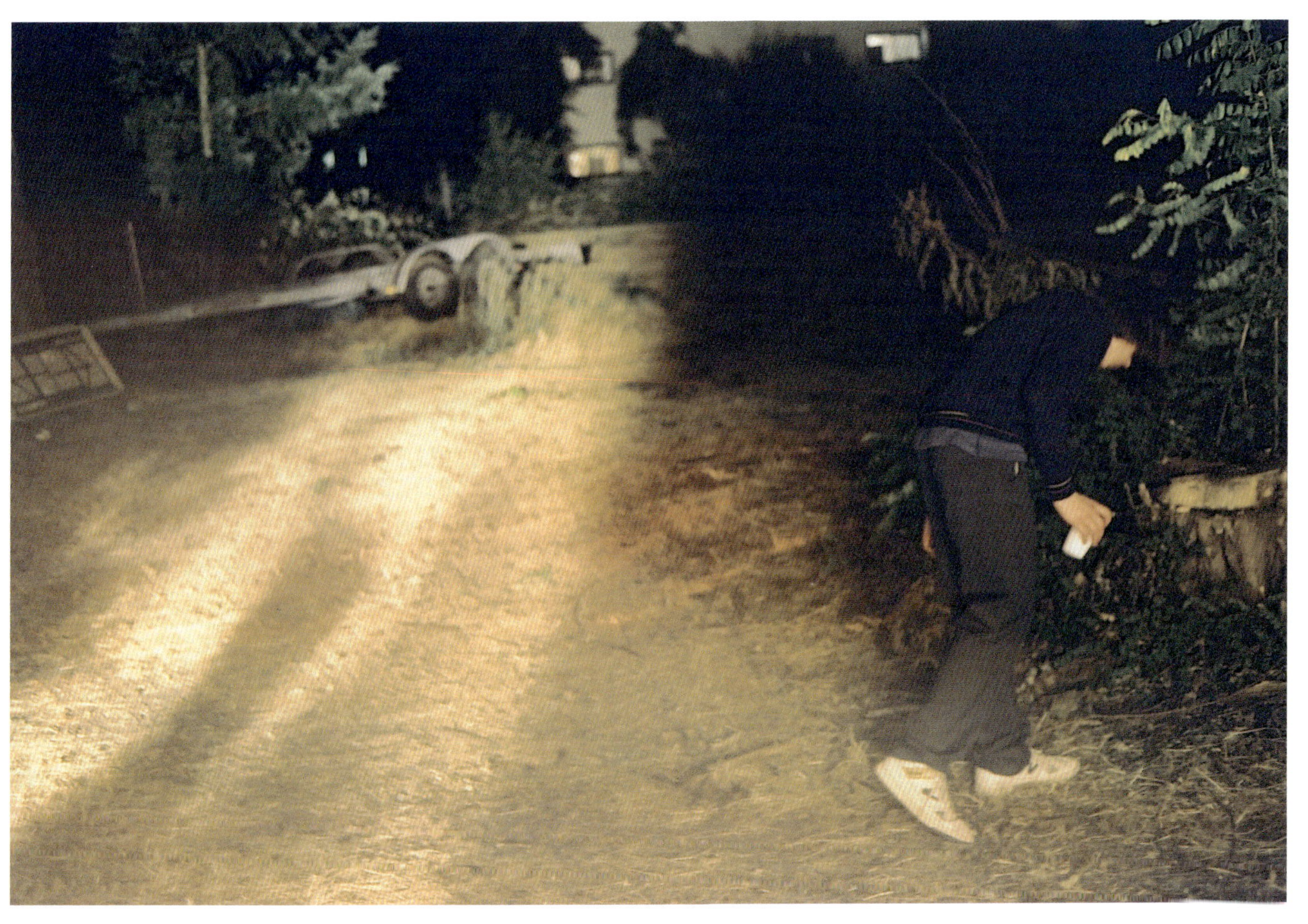

RM

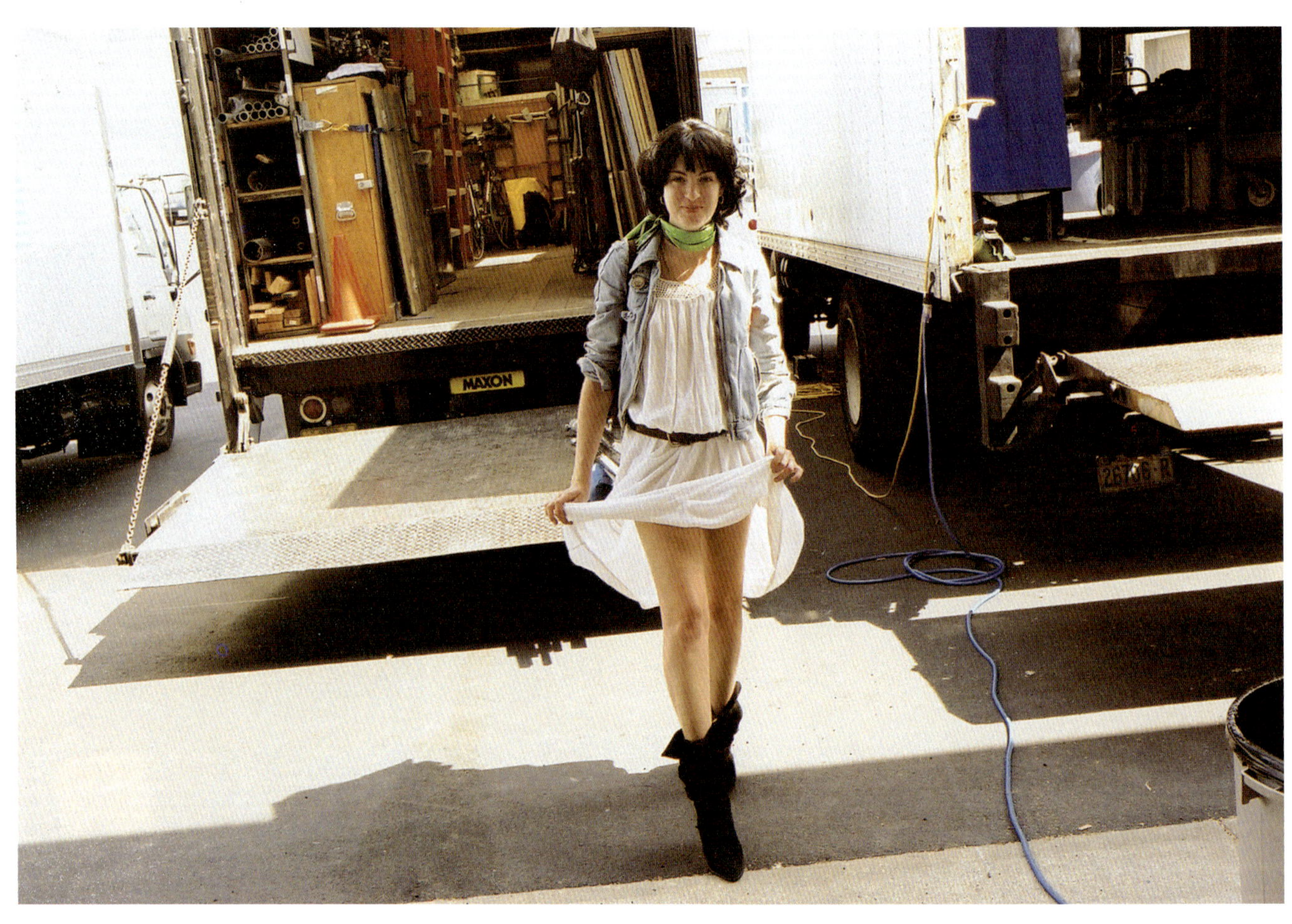

RM

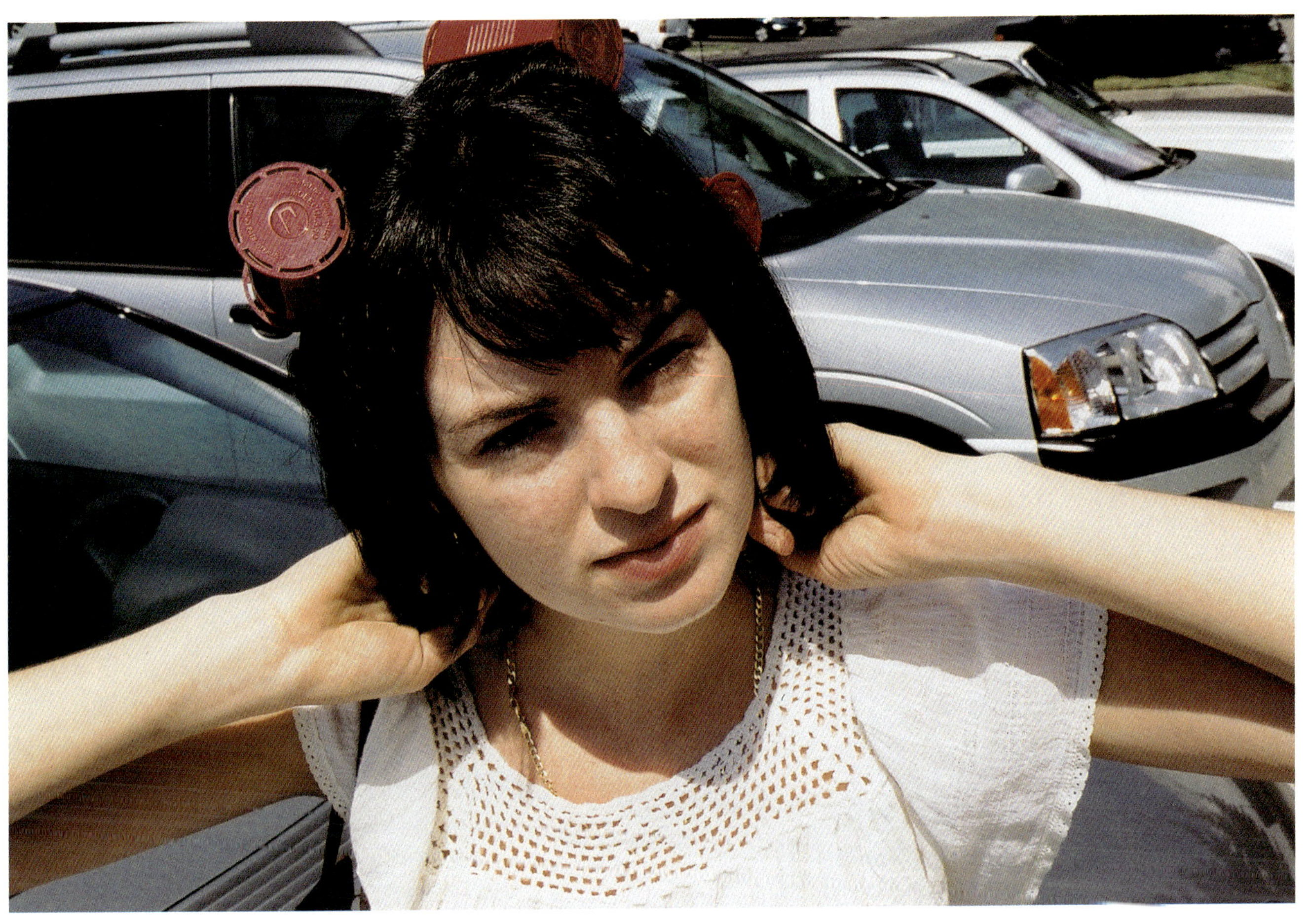

RM

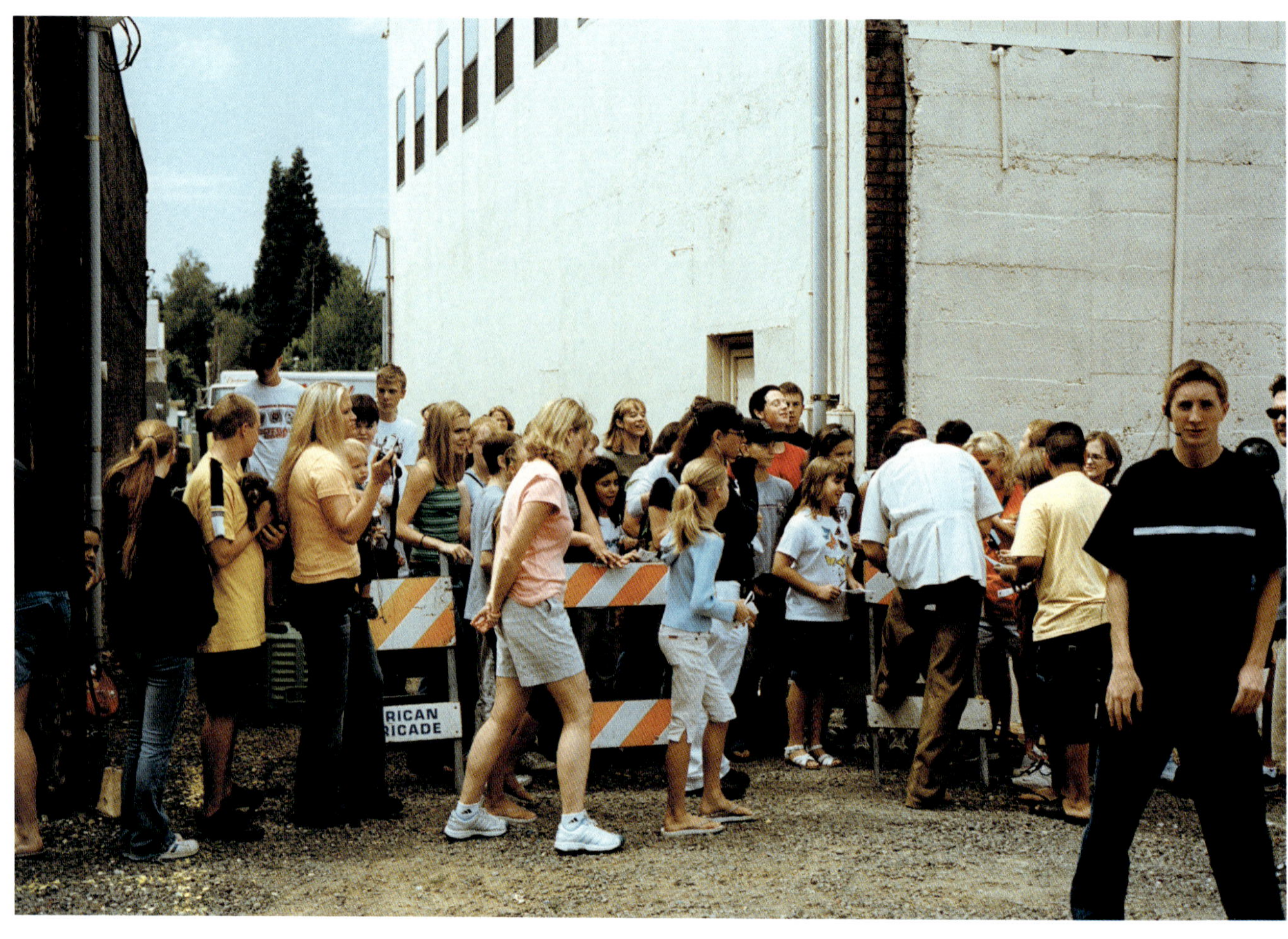

TC

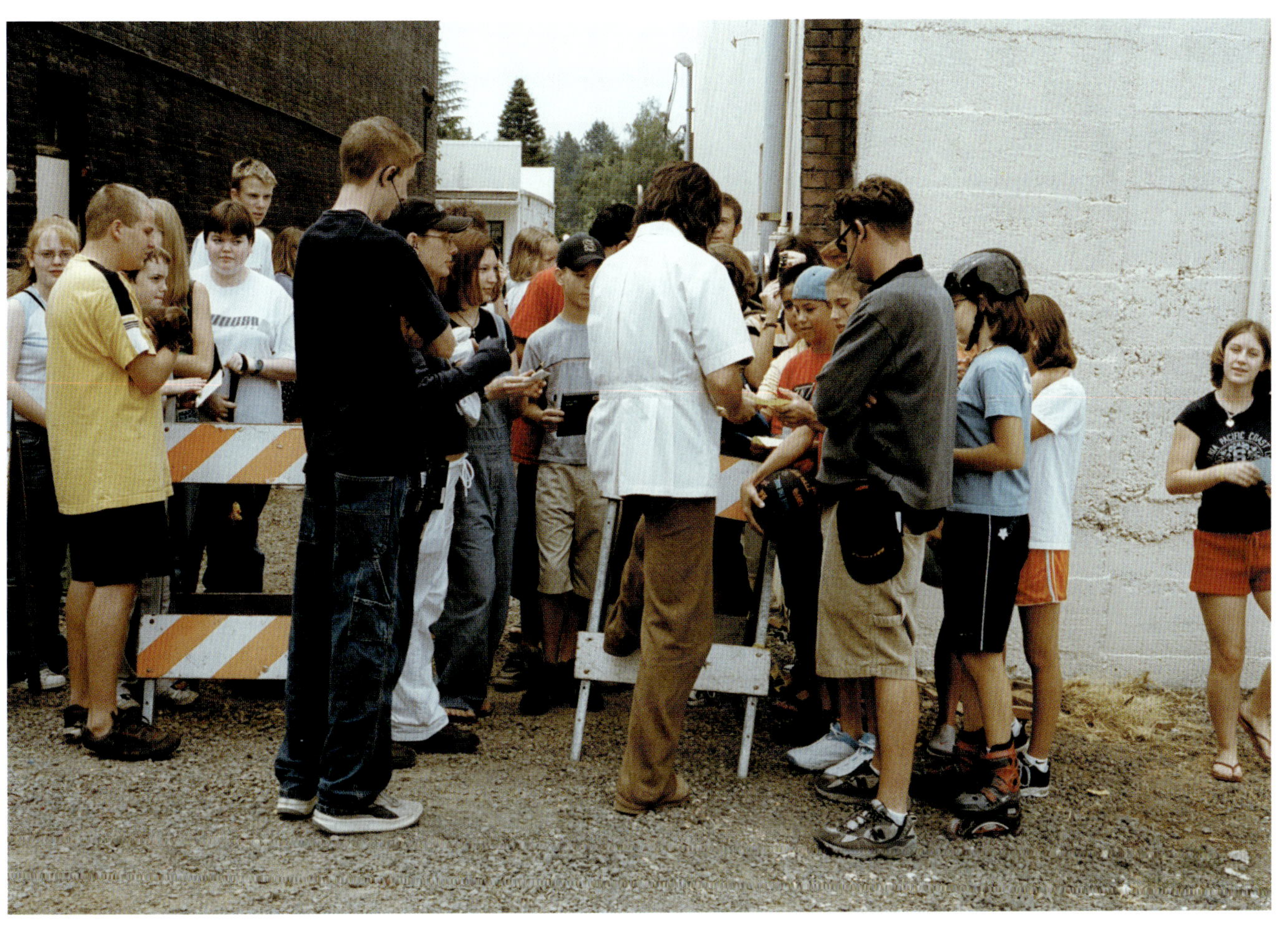

TC

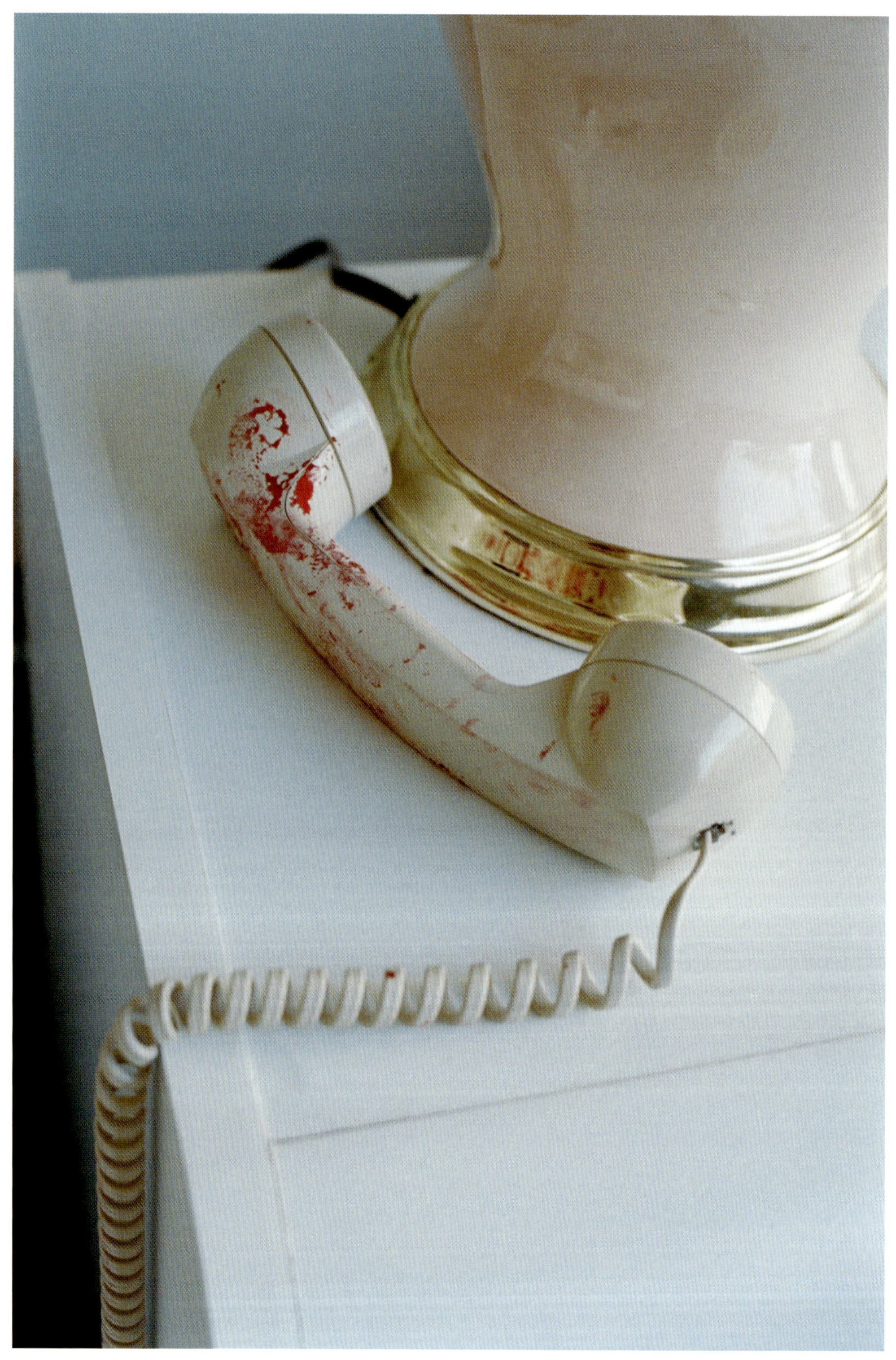

TC

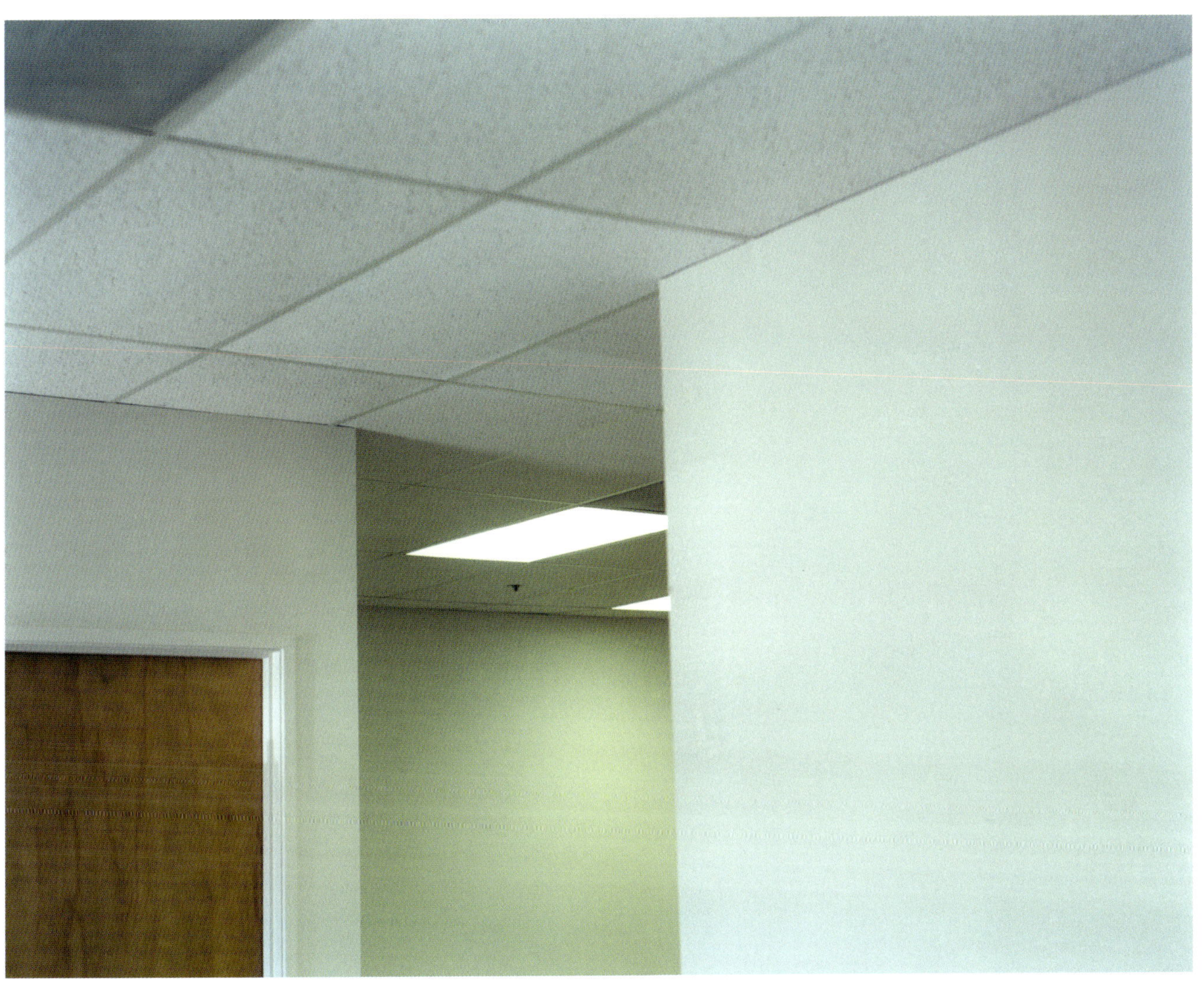

TC

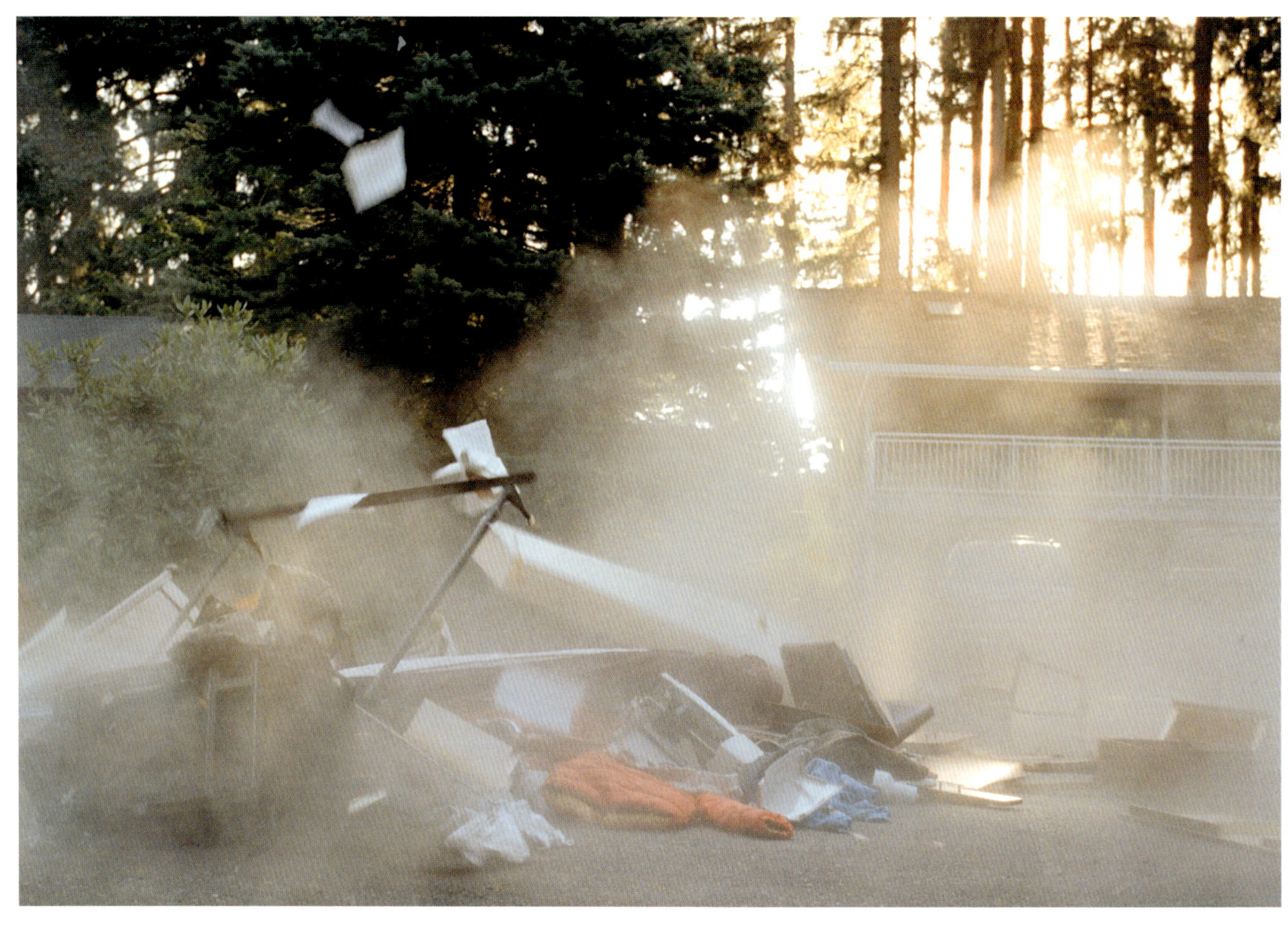

TC

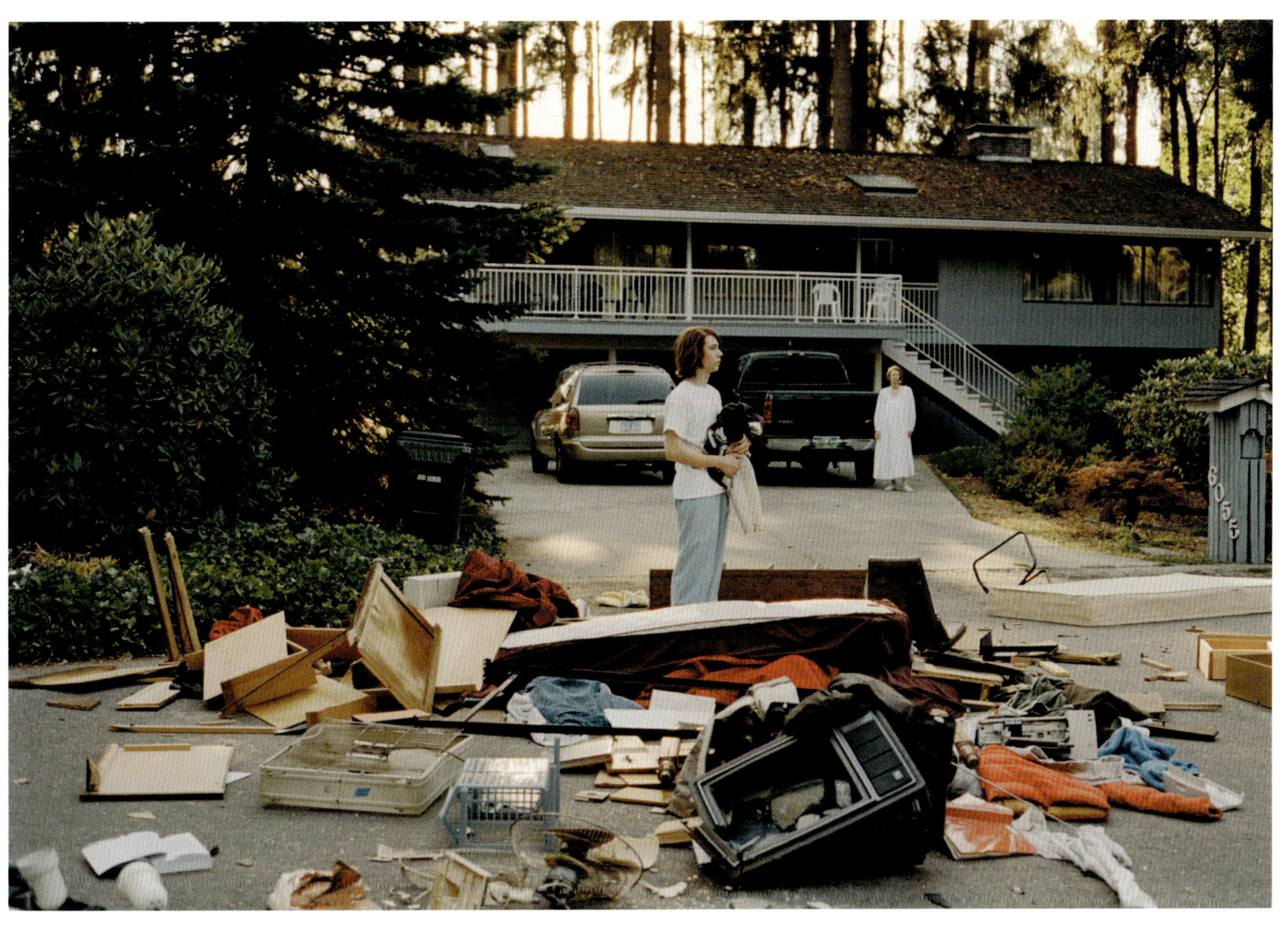

TC

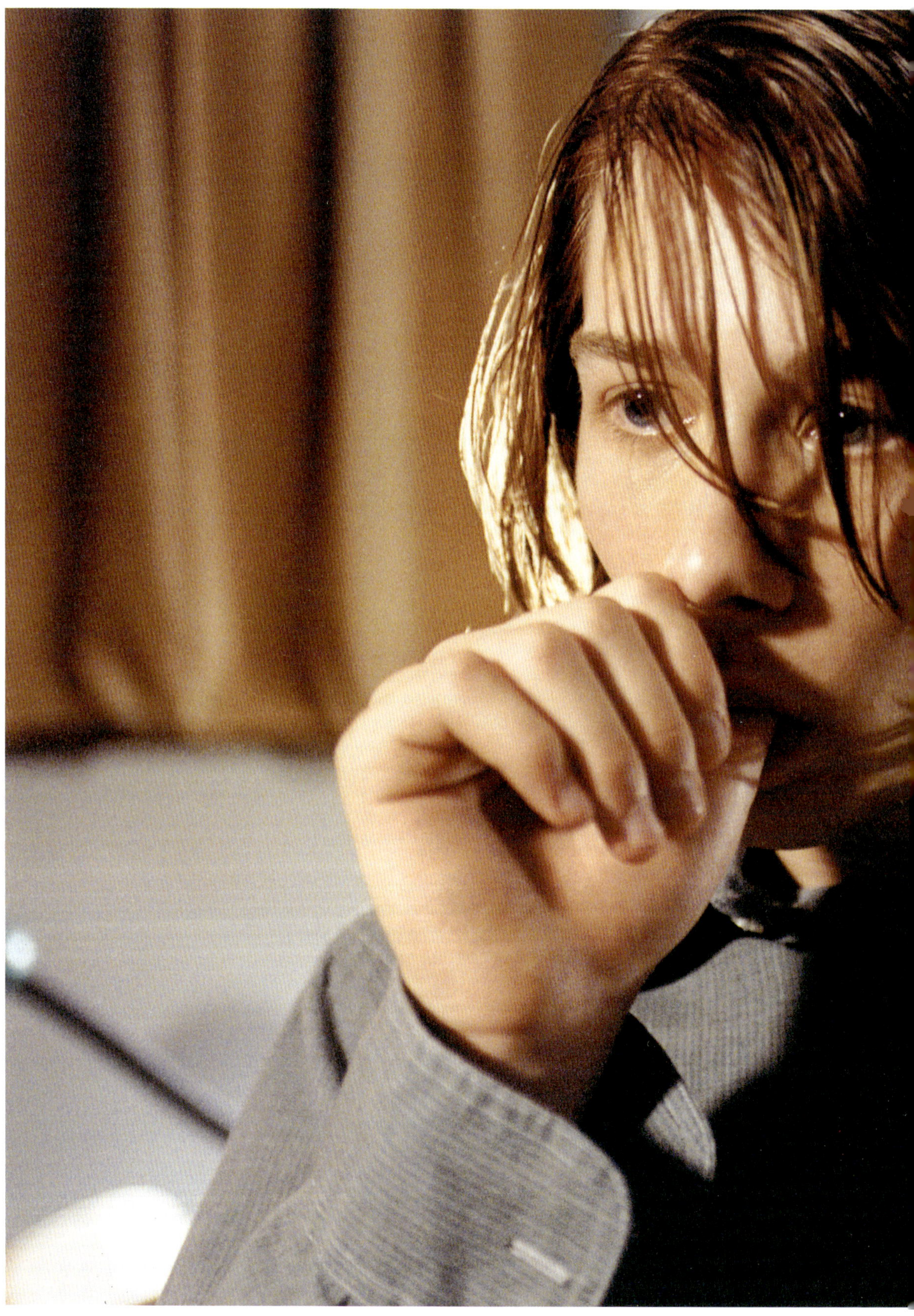

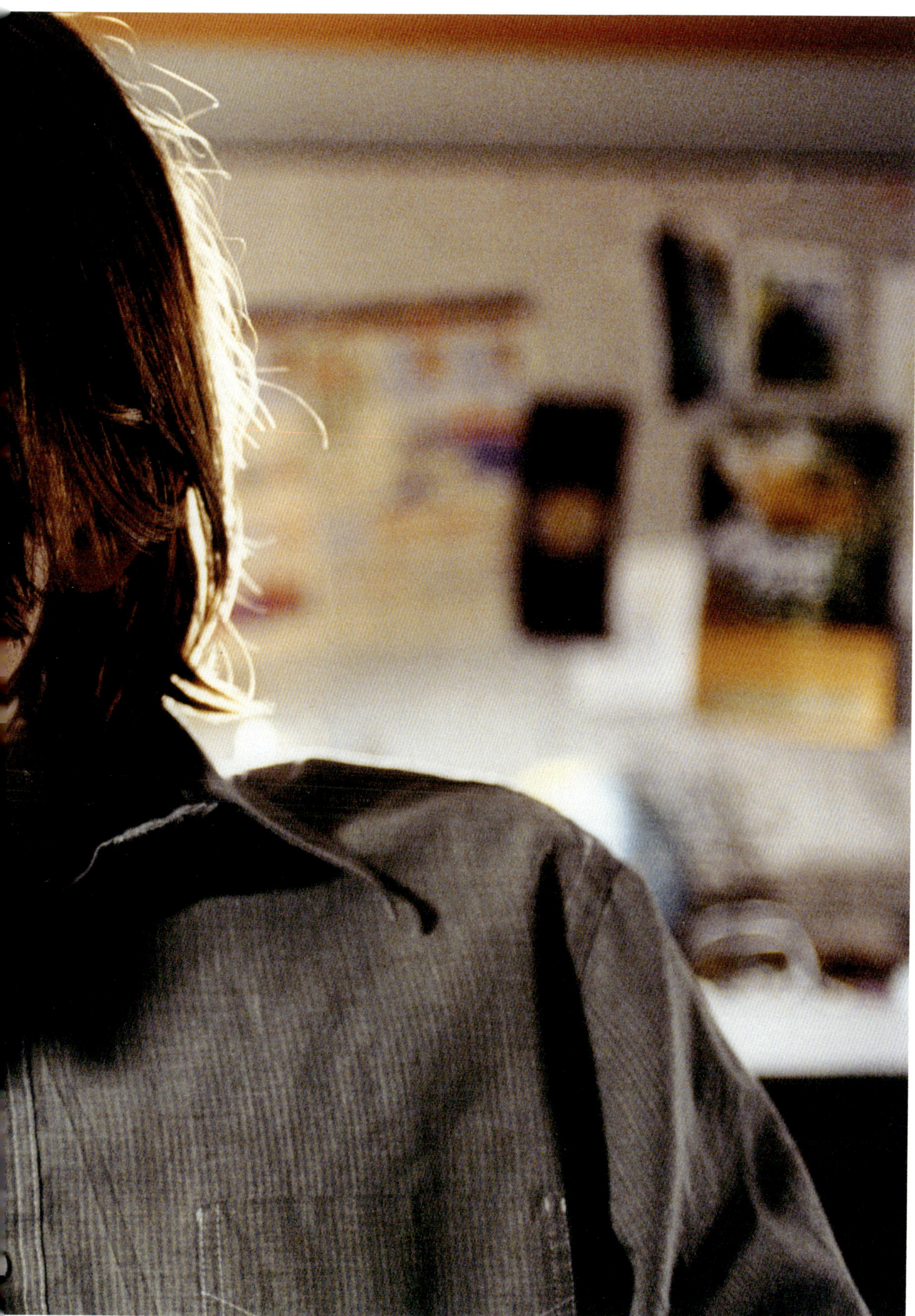

TC

AARON ROSE

At one point or another in life we have all felt like the world is against us. It's natural. One could even say that it is a necessary part of the human experience. If such a fact is true, however, then it is ironic that we hardly ever admit it. As modern societal beings, there is immense pressure placed on us to act well adjusted, in control, and on the right path. It is rare though that any of us really ever feel that way inside. Let's face it...none of us truly knows where we're going or how to get there. We spend a lot of time trying though. The world's religions are almost entirely based on giving us some semblance of life as a divine plan...and maybe they're not wrong. Most of the time, however, in the opinion of this writer, our entire existence is nothing more than a series of happy accidents.

What does all this have to do with Mike Mills? Well, everything really. For the last decade, through various mediums including fine art, design, music and films, Mills has been stumbling down the path of creativity, falling into projects and situations that have not only altered his own personal course, but significantly affected the actual disciplines he has employed as well. The notion of taking the long way around, the road less traveled while walking blind all the way has been integral to his career path. Ironically, from an outsider's glance, Mills' journey looks completely planned. However, one need only look deeper into the messages in his work to understand that in fact the exact opposite is true. Mike Mills is a searcher. He is an artist who travels this lost highway of life erecting metaphorical billboards (art) along the way announcing particular signposts on his own personal creative journey.

I first met Mike Mills in 1993 when he was a recent graduate of the design program at Cooper Union in New York. He was pretty much exclusively a graphic designer then. One of the first things I noticed about his work was that it was never simply about design. His works always held significant emotional content. For our first project together, Mills painted a highly graphic portrait of a young Mick Jagger on the back wall of the gallery. The surrounding walls were covered with framed prints designed to mimic the styles of various graphic movements popular throughout the 20th Century. Some looked psychedelic, some looked like Blue Note jazz albums, and some looked like heavy metal logos. Within each of these images were bold, colorful, sometimes typographically obscured renditions of the word "Help."

This project was an interesting precursor to so much of Mills' later oeuvre because in the simplest fashion what he was saying in that exhibition has been much the same ever since. Help. We all need it. No matter what style, shape or size we are as people, one thing is evidently clear. We need help. Help to get through the day, help to get through the night, help to get through life. The interesting thing about that particular show is perhaps not the sentiment, but the unique way in which Mills packaged it. When one walked into the gallery their first impression was that incredibly cool, ten foot high painting of Mick Jagger. It was bold, sexy and inviting. From a distance all the posters looked almost like tragically hip decorations for someone's trendy modernist home. However, upon closer inspection it was obvious that what we were looking at was not all about eye candy.

All of this color, style and uber-hipsterism was in fact a visual trick that Mills used to lure the viewer in, coax them to let down their guard in order to deliver his one-two emotional punch. It is perhaps Mills' greatest gift as an artist and something in his work that is more often than not overlooked.

Mike Mills' journey into the world of feature films has been indirect at best. In fact it has been downright roundabout. In those years following the "Help" exhibition, Mills went on to design album covers for many of the most acclaimed musicians of the time. His entrance to that world came accidentally in the form of an introduction to Kim Gordon of Sonic Youth through a friend who worked at a local skateboard shop. Gordon was looking for a designer for her then budding X-Girl fashion line and Mills happened to be a skateboarder who hung around the shop. That chance meeting led Mills to design record covers for musicians such as the Beastie Boys, Sonic Youth, Beck and the Jon Spencer Blues Explosion. For a moment he was the "it" designer in New York. I remember at one point in the mid-nineties walking by Tower Records on Broadway and noticing that a good majority of the album cover art, blown up into big light boxes in their windows, was designed by him. To any outsider, exposure on that level would indicate that Mike Mills had arrived. It was a young graphic designer's dream...but for Mills that wasn't the case at all. It's not that Mills was ungrateful for this particular time in the design limelight; it was just that in his mind, that signpost had been planted and it was time to move on...both literally and figuratively.

Soon after, he packed up his small design studio on Broadway and headed west to Los Angeles. It was a surprising move, but in retrospect made perfect sense. Before leaving New York, Mills had already made a few small forays into the medium of film. Amongst others, he directed a short film for jazz musician Ornette Coleman, a promotional film for fashion designer Marc Jacobs, and a short documentary titled *Deformer* about the life of professional skateboarder and artist Ed Templeton. For Mills to pursue this medium seriously, however, he would have to be on the West Coast. While couch surfing in Los Angeles, Mills began picking up music video and commercial work whenever he could, many times directing videos for the same musicians he had done graphic design work for while in New York. He eventually joined with fellow young director Roman Coppola to form an agency called The Directors Bureau.

Many who knew him thought it odd that someone like Mills, who had become such a figure on the pop cultural scene would sell out his rock and roll credibility to direct advertisements for Volkswagen and The Gap. Projects like these seemed the complete antithesis of what he was doing before, but it never fazed Mills. He looked at these projects in a much different light. Mills was a design student and never went to film school, so not only were these companies helping him survive as he set himself up on the West Coast, they were in effect paying him to learn the medium.

While continuing to direct music videos and commercials, Mills began to explore filmmaking more seriously. He directed his first narrative short, *The Architecture of Reassurance* in 1999, the documentary *Paperboys* in 2000, as well as more experimental projects created specifically for galleries. One of these films, *Honesty Shoes Love And Hair*, saw him interviewing various different people from all walks of life on the subjects mentioned in the title. The answers were then randomly assembled in the editing room without reference to their subject and the end result proved a telling portrait of the sometimes misguided priorities of human nature. While all of Mike Mills' early film work bore telltale signs of an overall aesthetic, it is perhaps these experimental works that reveal the most about his process and motivations. There is something in the simplicity and emotional content of these works that borders on psychotherapy. It is almost as if through these films; he was not only trying to make sense of the world around him, but of his own inner psyche as well. This brings us back to the notion of "Help."

Fast forward a few years to Mills' first feature film, *Thumbsucker*, the project to which the photographs in this book are dedicated. The film focuses on a group of characters that one could say are all in desperate need of assistance. Some seek it through religion, some through rehab, some through dentistry, but all of them are searching. They seek love, they seek acceptance but even more importantly, they strive for a place and identity within the world. They are confused by life and through a series of wrong turns they somehow find their way. Like that early mural of Mick Jagger, *Thumbsucker* lures the viewer in with beautiful imagery and celebrity names, but again it is only a trick. Once we're inside, we are forced to share the struggles of these characters. Unless you are an incredibly well adjusted human being, it is impossible not only to empathize with them, but somehow relate their conditions to your own life. The themes are just too central to the human experience to be ignored.

One can't help but draw parallels to Mills' trajectory as an artist. As you thumb (pardon the pun) through this book and take in the photographs, remember that they are only clues to the deeper story within. Try to look at this book as a dysfunctional family album of sorts: a collection of visual souvenirs created by a group of extremely talented people that serves as a document of a peculiar journey...a very human story that relates not only to the making of a wonderful film, but a portrait of an artist who, through a series of happy accidents, may have finally found his way.

MIKE MILLS

How did this happen?

The photographers in this book are all people I've been lucky enough to meet and get to know over the years. In different ways, all of their work influenced me while I dreamt up what *Thumbsucker* would look like. It seemed like a weird perfect circle to ask those people to come and take pictures while we were shooting. I didn't ask them to photograph the set or our actors or anything at all really. Most came just for a couple of days, only Todd Cole was there for the whole shoot - that's why there are so many of his photos.

I met Takashi almost 10 years ago. I had seen his book *Babyland* and I was taken by how it played with innocence and false innocence or an innocence that only exists in your mind as you walk through a complicated world. We worked on a book called *Baby Generation* with Sofia Coppola, and then I designed his book *Hyper Ballad* about Icelandic suburbs. I have been influenced by the weird distancing Takashi achieves in his photos, especially his photos of suburbia. They are so dry and sort of obvious they make this very common world feel abstract and alien. Through his eyes, the manmade world looks like a mistake that just got way out of hand. The great promise of Suburbia (everything will be okay) feels not just false, but sad and nostalgic, like, "Wasn't it nice when we actually could believe that?"

I first met Mark Borthwick about 7 years ago when he had a show in the back of Aaron Rose's Alleged Gallery and I had a show called *Honesty Shoes Love And Hair* in the front. I had known Mark's work and was jealous of how much he could get out of a picture of a simple little seedling tree. Mark's work constantly reminds me how simple you can be, and how simple can be very emotional. While there are many photographers taking pictures of the debris of our lives, the inanimate objects, lonely and alienated stuff (and I'm a sucker for that), Mark's photos have influenced me in the way he's looking for the positive and the spiritual in this debris. Mark seems to be able to see how everything is actually vibrating, how the inanimate is animated.

I also met Ed Templeton through the Alleged Gallery about 10 years ago. I did one of my first films, *Deformer*, about Ed and his wife Deanna and their push and pull relationship with Huntington Beach. It seems to me that Ed likes to live in a world totally unlike his work. His art is about admitting his darker thoughts, his weaknesses, his limitations, his bruises, his fucked-up-ness, and Huntington is the land that says, "None of that exists," and if you feel bad it's because you're flawed. Somehow Ed thrives off that contradiction. Maybe I can relate coming from Santa Barbara and from a world that says that everything is okay when it's not. That Ed has made those contradictions and duplicities the center of his work has influenced me a lot and inspired me to make the most out of my own personal mess.

Ryan McGinley popped up at some club one night in NY and gave me a copy of his book with a nice note inside. I loved how un-precious his photos were, how much fun it looked like he was having, and how messy everything seemed. The wall between the photographer and the subject felt blurred, and in a way, the photos seemed more about the activity that was happening than the end photo – which is so refreshing. It's mostly the mess and the energy in them that influenced me, and how they feel so un-nostalgic.

Todd Cole and I have collaborated over the years on a series of spray painting photos. Todd's work seems to be looking at the negotiation between the natural world and the manmade world, which is also a sub-theme of *Thumbsucker*. I think he is looking at how humans try to frame nature, to tame it, control it, and make it less scary and how nature fights back. Nature messes up our clean predictable world. Todd and I have often talked about that great William Eggleston quote from his book *Democratic Forest* where he says he's, "At war with the obvious." To me, that means he's at war with control. I think Todd is often photographing the border where our control just isn't working anymore – that's a place I always find inspiring.

THUMBSUCKER
PHOTOGRAPHY FROM THE FILM BY MIKE MILLS
MARK BORTHWICK
TODD COLE
TAKASHI HOMMA
RYAN MCGINLEY
ED TEMPLETON

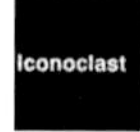

Published By Iconoclast
www.iconoclastusa.com

Design By Tim Koh, Mike Mills
Cover Design By Mike Mills

Printed in China
ISBN 0-9770610-0-0

A SONY PICTURES CLASSICS RELEASE BOB YARI PRODUCTIONS PRESENTS A THIS IS THAT CINEMA-GO-GO PRODUCTION IN ASSOCIATION WITH BULL'S EYE ENTERTAINMENT LOU PUCCI TILDA SWINTON VINCENT D'ONOFRIO KEANU REEVES BENJAMIN BRATT KELLI GARNER AND VINCE VAUGHN "THUMBSUCKER" CASTING BY JEANNE McCARTHY, C.S.A. LINE PRODUCER CALLUM GREENE MUSIC SUPERVISOR BRIAN REITZELL ORIGINAL MUSIC WRITTEN BY TIM DeLAUGHTER PERFORMED BY THE POLYPHONIC SPREE ADDITIONAL SONGS BY ELLIOTT SMITH COSTUME DESIGNER APRIL NAPIER EDITED BY ANGUS WALL AND HAINES HALL PRODUCTION DESIGNER JUDY BECKER DIRECTOR OF PHOTOGRAPHY JOAQUIN BACA-ASAY CO-EXECUTIVE PRODUCERS TILDA SWINTON JAY SHAPIRO EXECUTIVE PRODUCERS ANNE CAREY TED HOPE BOB YARI CATHY SCHULMAN PRODUCED BY ANTHONY BREGMAN BOB STEPHENSON BASED ON THE NOVEL BY WALTER KIRN WRITTEN AND DIRECTED BY MIKE MILLS

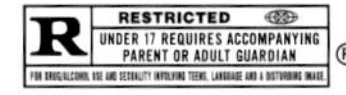

®

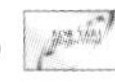

CINEMA-GO-GO

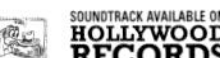

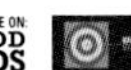

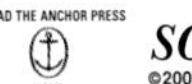

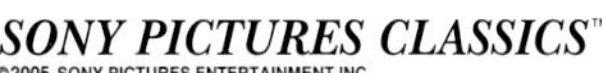

www.sonyclassics.com www.thumbsuckerthemovie.com

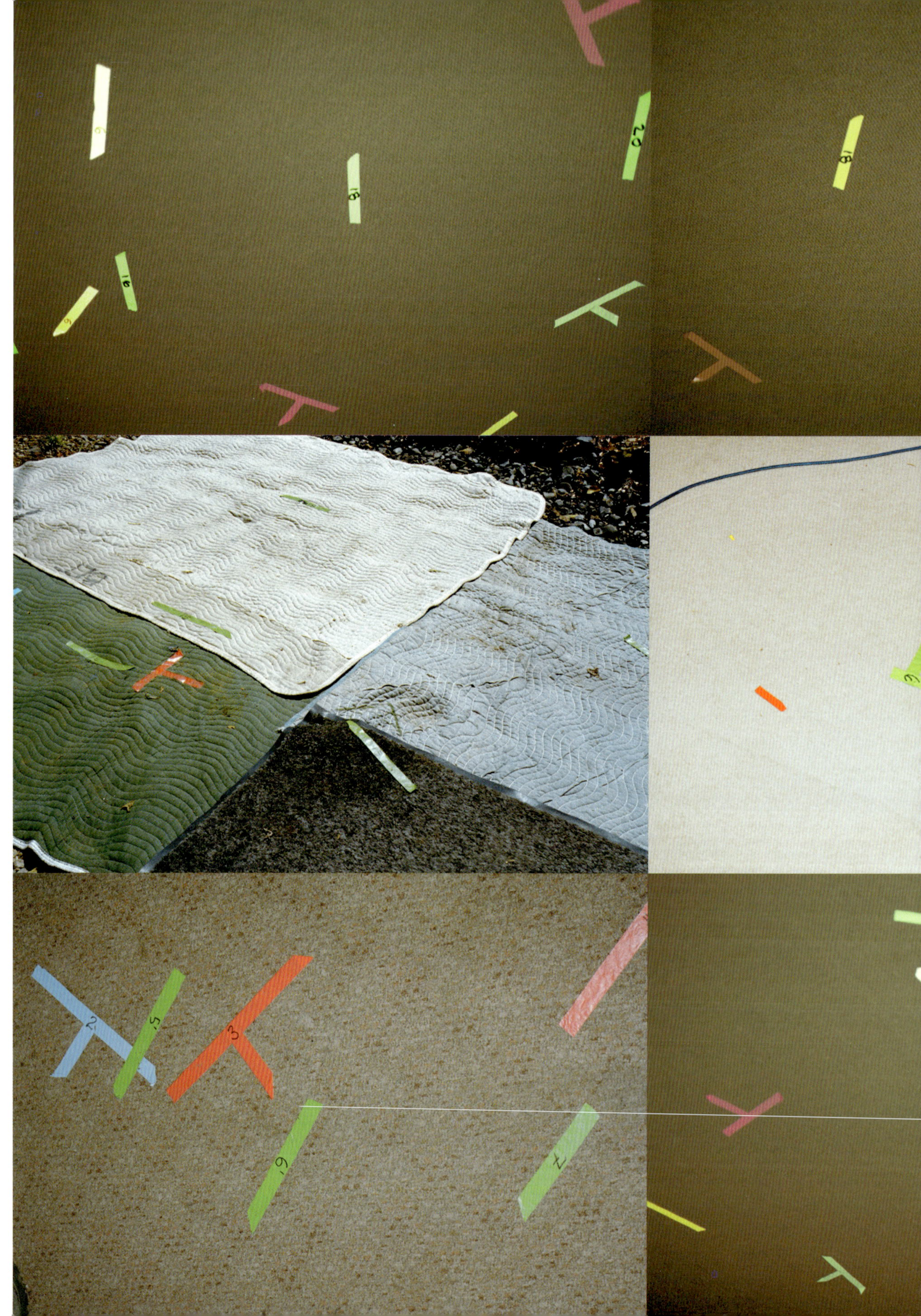

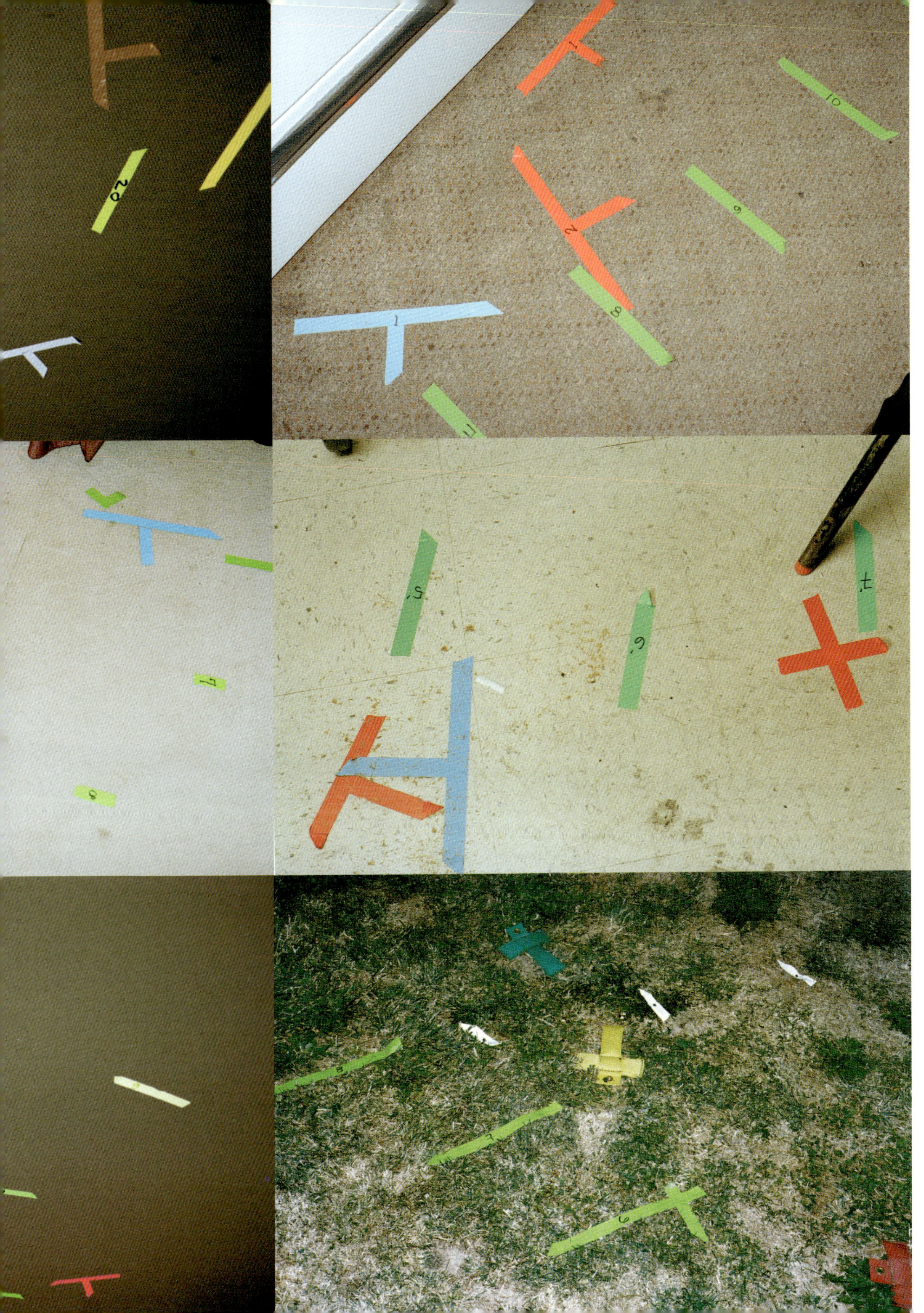

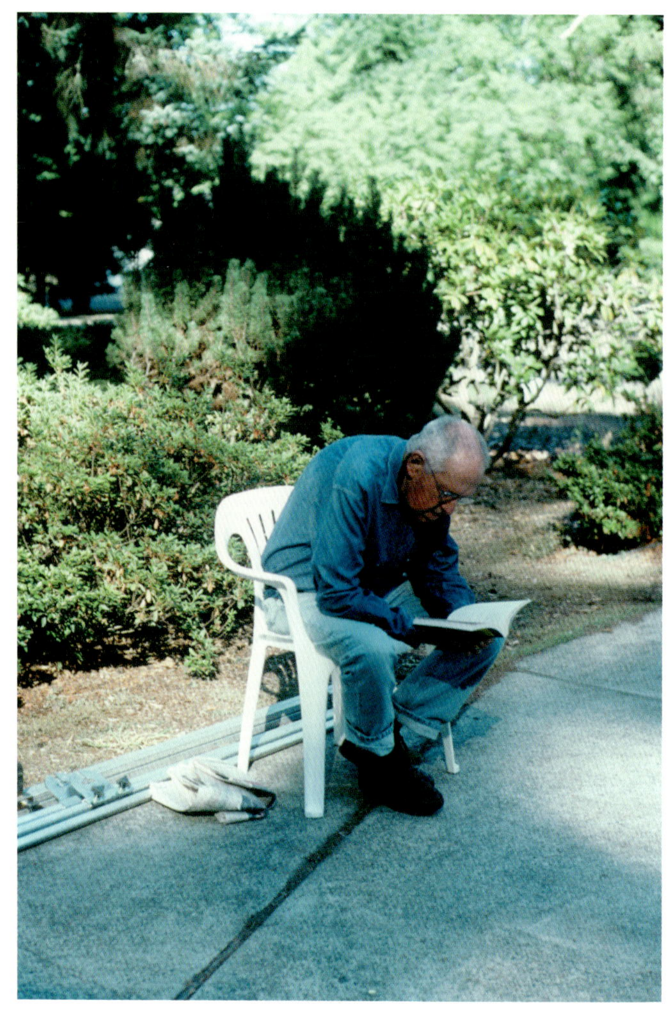

IN MEMORY OF PAUL CHADBOURNE MILLS

MB